QuickBooks Online Mastery

The Complete Beginner's Blueprint

ETHAN WELLS

TABLE OF CONTENTS

THANK YOU

Before we get started, I just want to say thank you for picking up this book. Whether you're a freelancer trying to make sense of your income and expenses, or a small business owner ready to finally feel in control of your finances—this book was written just for you.

I know accounting software can feel overwhelming at first. Maybe QuickBooks has been sitting on your to-do list for weeks (or months). Maybe you've tried other books that left you more confused than confident. That's exactly why I created this guide: to make QuickBooks Online feel doable, friendly, and approachable—even if you've never opened an accounting book in your life.

Bonus Tools Just for You

To help you hit the ground running, I've put together a collection of practical bonus resources you can download and use alongside this book. Don't forget to grab them at the end of this book.

Share the Love

If this book helped you feel more confident, saved you time, or simply made things click, would you mind leaving a quick review? It takes less than a minute, costs you nothing, and it can truly change an author's life. Honest reviews help more readers discover this guide, and they help me continue creating better, more helpful resources.

Scan the QR code below to share a review or tap the link (if you are reading the ebook):

Link

Enjoyed this book?

Explore more titles in the Business Productivity Blueprint series to continue building your skills and boosting your productivity. From mastering Excel and Word to managing your business with QuickBooks and Office 365, there's a guide for every step of your journey.

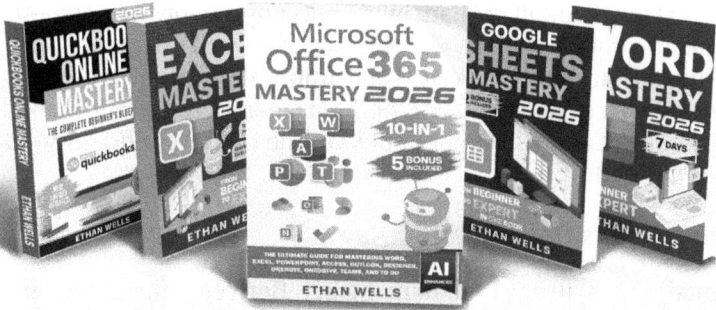

Scan the QR code below to access this series:

Something Not Quite Right?

If you run into any issues, feel something is missing, or have ideas to improve the next edition, I'm just an email away. Please tell me. I listen, and I care deeply about making things right.

Please reach out anytime at ethanwellsreads@gmail.com.

I genuinely want this book to be as helpful as possible, and your input makes all the difference.

Thanks again for trusting me as your guide. I'm wishing you every success as you take control of your business finances—one step, one click, one smart decision at a time.

With gratitude,

Ethan Wells

INTRODUCTION

Welcome to QuickBooks Online Mastery: The Complete Beginner's Blueprint—your go-to guide for getting comfortable with business finances, even if the very idea of accounting makes you break out in a cold sweat.

If you're a freelancer, a brand-new small business owner, or someone who's just tired of sorting through spreadsheets and hoping for the best—this book was made specifically for you. It's written for those with little to no background in bookkeeping or accounting. You won't find technical jargon or high-level financial strategy here. What you will find is a clear, easy-to-follow roadmap to help you understand and use QuickBooks Online (QBO) confidently—without feeling overwhelmed.

1. Why QuickBooks Online?

Running a business is already a balancing act. Between managing customers, handling services or products, and trying to stay profitable, it's easy to let bookkeeping slide. That's where QuickBooks Online shines—it simplifies your day-to-day financial tasks, automates tedious work, and helps you keep everything organized in one place.

And the best part? You don't need an accounting degree to use it. QBO is designed with real business owners in mind—people like you who are looking for a smarter, easier way to manage money.

2. Who This Book Is For

Let's be super clear: this book is for absolute beginners only.

Whether you're:

- A freelancer managing your own invoices for the first time,
- A solopreneur trying to keep business and personal finances separate,
- Or a small business owner wearing all the hats and trying to get a handle on cash flow...

This guide is your step-by-step companion.

No prior accounting experience? Perfect. Never touched QuickBooks before? Even better. Looking for something simple that actually makes sense? You're in the right place.

3. Who This Book Is Not For

This guide is not for advanced users, experienced accountants, or anyone seeking complex tax strategies, deep-dive financial analysis, or custom automation scripts. If you're already fluent in GAAP or reconciling journal entries in your sleep—this book probably isn't what you need.

4. What Makes This Book Different?

This isn't just a how-to manual. It's more like having a friendly coach by your side, showing you:

- Exactly what to click and why it matters
- How to apply everything directly to your business
- What to avoid so you don't waste time or make common rookie mistakes

You'll find:

- Plain English explanations (no accounting degree required)
- Beginner-focused examples relevant to real-world freelance and small business scenarios
- Checklists and summaries to help you stay on track

5. How to Use This Book

The best way to learn QuickBooks is to use it. So here's how to get the most out of this guide:

- Start at the beginning – Each chapter builds on the last. Don't skip ahead!
- Follow along in your own QBO account – Practice as you go to reinforce each lesson.
- Be patient with yourself – You're learning a new skill, and that's something to be proud of.
- Use the bonuses and checklists – We've included helpful tools throughout the book to keep you organized and confident.

By the time you finish, you'll know how to track income and expenses, send invoices, pay your team, manage inventory, and handle taxes with ease—all from your QuickBooks dashboard.

So take a deep breath, open up your QBO account, and get ready to turn those messy finances into a system that actually works.

Let's dive in—you've got this.

Chapter 1: Getting Started with QuickBooks Online

I. Understanding QuickBooks Online and Its Benefits

1. What is QuickBooks Online?

Imagine having your own personal assistant, tirelessly working behind the scenes to manage your bookkeeping, track expenses, and organize your financial reports—without ever needing a coffee break! That's essentially QuickBooks Online (or QBO, as we like to call it).

QuickBooks Online is a cloud-based accounting software designed specifically for small businesses, freelancers, and entrepreneurs just like you. Because it operates in the cloud, you can securely access your financial data anytime, anywhere, from any device with an internet connection.

2. Key Benefits for Small Businesses

Why choose QuickBooks Online for small businesses:

1. Ease of Use: QBO's user-friendly interface means you don't need an accounting degree to understand your finances.
2. Time-Saving Automation: Say goodbye to repetitive tasks. QuickBooks Online automates invoicing, expense tracking, bank reconciliation, and even payroll.
3. Financial Visibility: Clear, easy-to-understand dashboards and reports give you real-time insights into your financial health.
4. Anywhere, Anytime Access: Work from home, a café, or halfway across the globe. Your financial data stays accessible and secure.
5. Affordable and Scalable: Whether you're just starting out or scaling up, QBO grows with your business without breaking the bank.
6. Collaboration Simplified: Easily collaborate with your accountant or bookkeeper by giving them secure access.

Remember, the key to success isn't just working harder, but smarter—and QuickBooks Online helps you do exactly that!

II. Choosing the Right QuickBooks Plan

QuickBooks Online offers four distinct plans designed to suit businesses of different sizes and needs. Here's a quick overview to help you see where you might fit:

- Simple Start: Ideal for solo entrepreneurs or freelancers. It allows you to track income and expenses, send invoices, and run basic financial reports.
- Essentials: Perfect for small businesses needing more organization and control. It includes all features of Simple Start, plus bill management, support for multiple users, and time tracking.
- Plus: Great for growing businesses managing more complex operations. This includes everything in Essentials, plus inventory tracking, project profitability tracking, and more detailed reporting.
- Advanced: Best for larger, more sophisticated businesses needing robust customization and analytics. It provides all features of Plus, advanced reporting, dedicated account support, and additional automation tools.

1. Features Comparison Chart

Here's a friendly side-by-side look at the main features of each plan:

Features	Simple Start	Essentials	Plus	Advanced
Track Income & Expenses	Yes	Yes	Yes	Yes
Invoice & Accept Payments	Yes	Yes	Yes	Yes
Manage Bills	Yes	Yes	Yes	Yes
Multiple Users	1 User	3 Users	5 Users	25 Users
Track Time	No	Yes	Yes	Yes
Track Inventory	No	No	Yes	Yes
Advanced Reporting	No	No	No	Yes
Financial Planning	No	No	Yes	Yes

2. Determining the Best Fit for Your Business

Choosing the right QuickBooks plan doesn't have to feel overwhelming—just think about what your business really needs right now and where you plan to be in the next year or two. Here are some simple questions to help you:

1. How many users will need access to QuickBooks?
   » If it's just you, Simple Start could be perfect.
   » For small teams, consider Essentials or Plus.
2. Do you manage inventory or billable projects?
   » Plus or Advanced would be your best bet.
3. Are detailed analytics and reports important for your growth?
   » Advanced would provide the insights you need.
4. What's your budget?
   » Each tier offers great value, so choose the one aligning comfortably with your current budget while leaving room for growth.

Still not sure? Don't worry—QuickBooks allows you to upgrade seamlessly as your business evolves. What's more, QuickBooks offers free trial or discount from time to time, so make sure you check the latest promotion offer they have. With that settled, let's move forward and set up your QuickBooks Online account step-by-step.

III. Creating Your QuickBooks Online Account Step-by-Step

1. Account Registration Guide

Getting started with QuickBooks Online is very straight-forward and easy. Follow these simple steps to register your account:

1. Visit the QuickBooks website: Go to quickbooks.intuit.com and click on the "Sign up" or "Free trial" button.

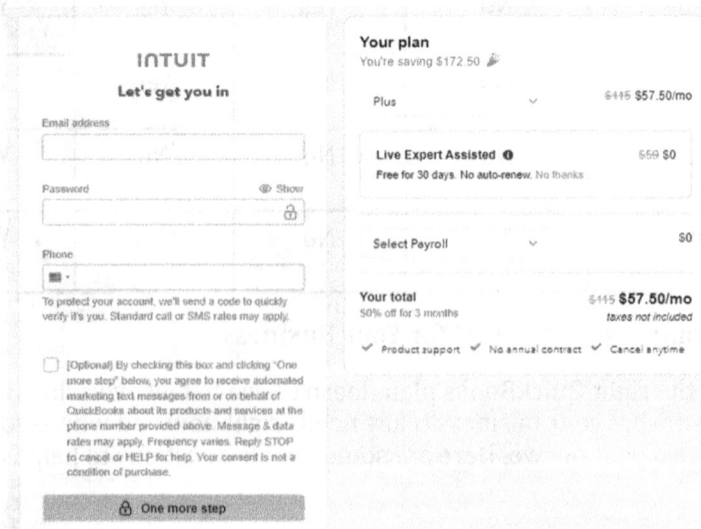

2. Choose your plan: Select the plan you've determined is best for your business—Simple Start, Essentials, Plus, or Advanced.

3. Enter your email: Provide a valid email address you'll use to log in regularly.

4. Create a password: Make sure your password is strong, unique, and memorable.

5. Provide your business information: Enter your business name, type of business, and other basic details as prompted.

6. Submit your information: Click the button to finalize your registration.

Congratulations, your QuickBooks account is officially alive!

2. Initial Account Setup

Now let's customize your account, making it truly yours.

Log into QuickBooks

Use your new credentials to log in. In the first time logging in, QuickBooks will ask you to set up your name, additional security to your account.

Enter information

As you navigate through the setup, QuickBooks will prompt you to enter details such as your business name and any prior accounting software you've used. If you've been managing your books using spreadsheets or another accounting program, QuickBooks offers data migration options to help you get a head start. For illustration purposes, here's the sample business information we'll use throughout this guide:

- Company name: EverBloom Services
- Industry: Event Planning & Floral Design
- Owner: Ethan Wells
- Accounting History: Just starting to use an accounting software.

QuickBooks asks for your business name, industry, and structure. For EverBloom Services, we selected "Other" for industry and "Private Limited Company" as the business structure. These details help QuickBooks tailor features to your needs.

Tell us more about EverBloom Services

This info will help us make better suggestions for your business.

Industry (optional)

> Other   ⌄

Can you tell us what you do specifically?

> Event Planning & Floral Design

Begin entering your industry and select the option that fits best.

Business structure - Select the most relevant option - LLC isn't shown here because it could be created alongside other business types (e.g. sole proprietor as a single member LLC)

> Private limited company   ⌄

Next, specify your role and how many people work in your business. We chose "Owner or partner" and "10–24 employees" to reflect a growing team.

Initial setup

QuickBooks then suggests three setup tasks: link a bank account or personalize invoices. For this example, we will start with personalizing invoice template.

In this step, QuickBooks Online allows you to change the color theme and upload your logo to your invoice template. For further customization, you can make additional adjustments in the Products section.

Personalize your invoice template

Make it as unique as you are. Further customization items for invoicing are in the product.

Pick a color theme   ^

Select from our options, or enter a specific color value.

#ff8c00

Upload your logo (optional)   ⌄

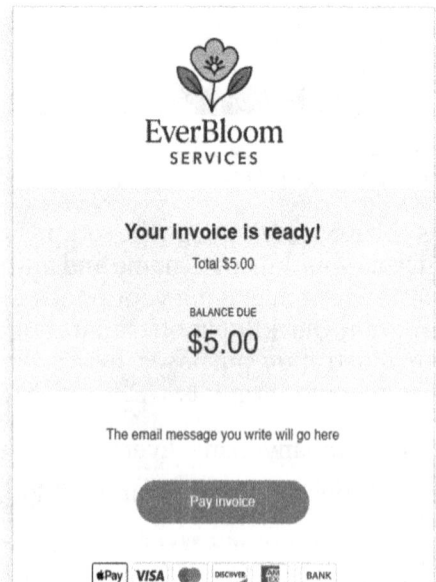

EverBloom
SERVICES

Your invoice is ready!

Total $5.00

BALANCE DUE

$5.00

The email message you write will go here

Pay invoice

⌗Pay VISA ● DISCOVER AMEX BANK

If you're using the Plus or Advanced plan along with Payroll Core, you can begin setting up your team's personal information and payroll. However, for this simple setup, we'll skip that step for now.

You also have the option to link your bank accounts at this stage. While this is a valuable feature, we'll hold off for now so we can explore the full benefits of bank connections in a later section.

In this step you are suggested to download the QBO app from AppStore or Google Play so that you can snap and save receipts from anywhere. This is extremely handy since the app will automatically detect and write down the details of receipts for you, you only need to review and approve them.

All settings can be adjusted or updated anytime once you're logged into your account, so don't worry if everything isn't perfect right now. In Chapter 2, we'll take a closer look at the essential setup steps in detail.

Up next, we'll guide you through navigating your new QuickBooks Online dashboard and menus with confidence.

IV. Navigating Your QBO Dashboard and Menus

1. Understanding the Dashboard Layout

Now that your account is set up, it's time to get comfortable inside QuickBooks Online. This section will help you understand what you're seeing on screen, where to click, and how to move around with confidence—without feeling overwhelmed.

Understanding the Dashboard Layout

When you land on the QuickBooks Online dashboard, you'll notice a row of common apps near the top of the screen. QuickBooks now organizes most of your work by apps, not menus. Each app represents a major area of your business and groups related actions together.

Not all apps appear on every plan. For example, Projects and Inventory are available on Plus and Advanced plans. If you don't see an app, it usually means your plan doesn't include that feature.

Company Identity

At the top of your interface, you'll see your company name and logo (if uploaded), which instantly confirms you're working in the right file. This personal touch also appears on your invoices and reports.

Create Actions

Just below the Apps bar, you'll see Create actions. These are quick shortcuts for the most common things business owners do, such as: Create invoice, Record expense, Add bank deposit or Create cheque.

If you click Show all, QuickBooks reveals even more options.

Think of Create actions as your fast lane. When you already know what you want to do, this is often the quickest way to get there.

Business at a Glance: Your Financial Snapshot

The center of the dashboard is the Business at a glance section. This area gives you a high-level overview of your business without requiring you to run reports. Typical widgets include:

- Profit & Loss – A snapshot of income, expenses, and net profit
- Expenses – A visual summary showing where your money is going
- Bank Accounts – Prompts to connect your bank and view balances
- Cash Flow – A forward-looking chart based on linked bank transaction.

Each widget is interactive. Clicking on it takes you to more detailed information.

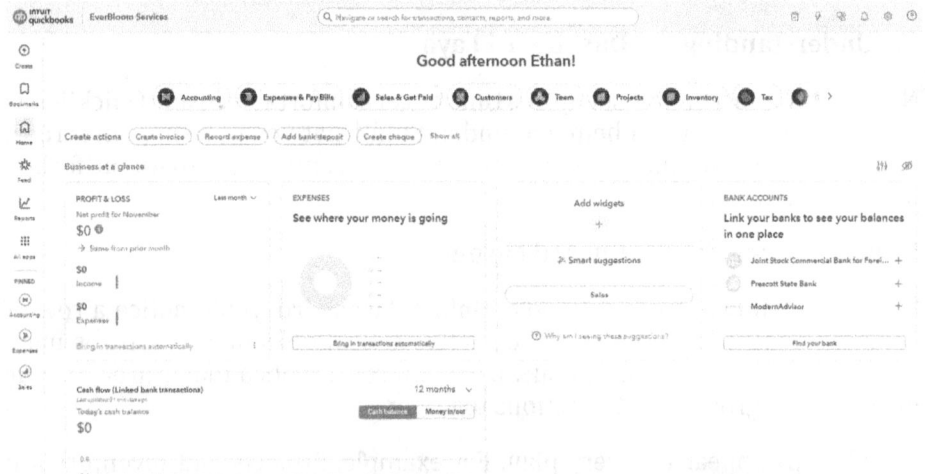

2. Customizing Your Dashboard View

QuickBooks allows you to customize what appears on your dashboard so it matches how you run your business. You'll see an Add widgets box with a plus (+) icon. From here, you can:

- Add or remove widgets
- Rearrange them
- Accept Smart suggestions based on your activity.

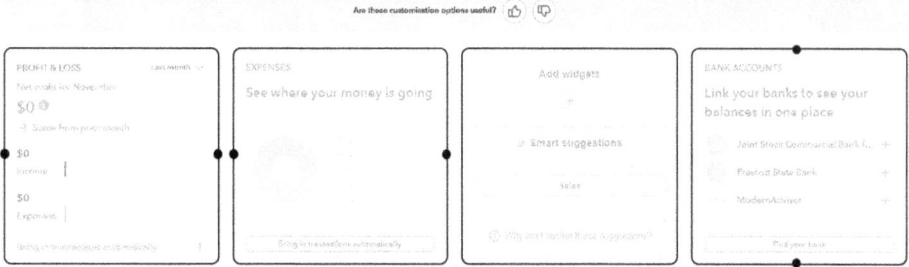

You can revisit this layout anytime as your business grows or your focus shifts. Think of your dashboard as your mission control panel—it should show you exactly what you need, when you need it.

3. Navigation Bar and Pinned Apps

On the left-hand side of the screen is the sidebar navigation, made up of icons rather than long text menus. Key sections include:

- Home – Returns you to the main dashboard
- Feed – Shows recent activity and automated actions
- Reports – Access all financial and management reports
- All apps – A complete list of apps and tools in one place
- Bookmarks – Quick access to pages you've saved
- Create (+) – Another way to add transactions quickly

You can pin your most-used apps to this sidebar navigation for quick access by clicking the Customize button and pin your apps.

Customise your app menus

Drag and drop to reorder apps, and pin your top apps for easy access.

- Accounting
- Expenses & Pay Bills
- Sales & Get Paid
- Customer Hub
- Team
- Project Management
- Inventory
- Tax

Reset to default   Cancel   Save

4. Feed: Reviewing Activity and AI-Suggested Work

The Feed area is newer and easy to overlook, but it's worth understanding.

Here you can find work done by Intuit's AI agents to help you decide and take action on what matters most. The Feed can help with many business tasks, such as:

- Matching bank transactions.
- Sending payment reminders for overdue invoices.
- Generating bills from emails.
- Alerting you to cash flow issues.
- Suggested items or tasks for you to review.

5. All Apps: Finding Everything in One Place

If you ever feel lost, click All apps in the left sidebar. This opens a panel showing:

- Accounting
- Expenses & Bills
- Sales & Get Paid
- And other available apps

V. Securely Accessing QuickBooks Across Multiple Devices

Now that you're confidently navigating your dashboard, let's ensure you can seamlessly and securely access your QuickBooks Online (QBO) account, whether you're at your desk, at home, or even on-the-go. After all, the beauty of QuickBooks Online is its flexibility—your finance is always within reach.

1. Setting Up Mobile and Tablet Access

One of the biggest perks of QuickBooks Online is the ability to access your data from virtually anywhere, right from your smartphone or tablet. Here's how you can quickly set up mobile and tablet access:

1. Download the QuickBooks Online App:
   » Visit the Apple App Store for iOS devices or Google Play Store for Android devices.
   » Search for "QuickBooks Online."
   » Download and install the official QuickBooks Online app.
2. Log In to Your Account:
   » Open the QuickBooks app on your device.
   » Enter the same username and password you use for your web-based QBO account.
3. Enable Notifications (Optional):
   » Once logged in, you'll have the option to enable notifications.
   » Notifications keep you instantly updated about invoices, payments, or other important financial activities.

Having QBO mobile access means your financial data travels with you wherever you go—talk about convenience!

2. Security Best Practices for Multi-Device Use

With great flexibility comes the important responsibility of ensuring your financial data remains secure. Here are some essential tips for keeping your QuickBooks account safe across multiple devices:

- Use Strong and Unique Passwords:
  » Create complex passwords combining letters, numbers, and special characters.
  » Avoid easily guessable passwords like "123456" or "password."
  » Regularly update passwords to enhance security.
- Activate Two-Factor Authentication (2FA):
  » Go to your QuickBooks security settings and enable two-factor authentication.
  » This adds an extra security layer by requiring a second form of verification, typically via your phone or email.
- Avoid Using Public Wi-Fi for Financial Transactions:
  » Always use trusted and secure internet connections when logging into QuickBooks.

- » If public Wi-Fi is your only option, consider using a reputable Virtual Private Network (VPN).

- Keep Your Devices Updated: Regularly update the QuickBooks app and your device's operating system to benefit from the latest security enhancements.
- Monitor Account Activity: Periodically check your account's audit log (available in QBO settings) to ensure no unauthorized activities occur.

Taking these simple precautions helps ensure your financial information stays safe, secure, and confidential.

3. Managing User Permissions and Accessibility

Chances are, you won't be the only person accessing your QuickBooks account. To ensure your team can work efficiently while maintaining strict security, QuickBooks provides an intuitive system to manage user permissions:

1. Access User Management:
   - » Click the Gear icon at the top right.
   - » Select Manage Users from the dropdown menu.

2. Adding New Users:
   - » Click on Add User. Enter the information of the person you're inviting.
   - » Select an existing role or create a new one.

3. Setting Permission Levels:
   - » Assign the appropriate access level (Administrator, Standard User, Reports Only, etc.).
   - » Tailor access further by granting permissions related specifically to the user's role (e.g., invoicing, expense tracking, payroll).

Add user

Enter personal info

We'll send them an invite to join your company with their Intuit Account.

First name   Last name   Email

Assign roles

Choose from existing roles or create your own. View role descriptions

Select a role   ⌄

> **View all permissions**

4. Monitoring and Adjusting Permissions:

- » Regularly review user access levels.
- » Adjust or revoke access as team roles and responsibilities change.

By thoughtfully managing user permissions, you empower your team to perform their tasks effectively without compromising your business's financial integrity.

Chapter 2: Essential QuickBooks Setup

I. Company Information

Now it's time to set up your company's essential information in QuickBooks Online. Think of this as laying a strong foundation for your business's financial house—solid foundations lead to smoother operations.

1. Navigate to Your Company Settings:

» Click on the Gear icon in the upper-right corner.

» Select **Account and Settings** under the "Your Company" section.

Settings				ⓘ
Company				
Usage				
Accounting				
Sales		**Company info**		
Expenses		This info may be used for billing purposes.		
Time				
Advanced		**Name**	EverBloom Services	Edit
		Address		Edit
		Email	ethanwellsreads@gmail.com	Edit
		Phone		Edit
		Website		Edit
		Industry	Event Planning & Floral Design	Edit

2. Enter Your Company Details:

» Under the Company tab, you'll enter essential details like your business name, industry type, and contact information.

» Provide your business's legal name, address, email, and phone number and industry.

» Scroll down to Legal info and edit tax form (Sole Proprietor, Partnership, or Corporation) and your tax ID number (EIN or SSN).

» Be sure to upload your business logo—it's a great personal touch that will appear on invoices and reports.

3. Save Your Information:

» Once everything looks correct, click Done, and you're all set!

By completing this step now, you're ensuring your reports, invoices, and tax filings all reflect accurate and professional business information—no cleanup required later..

II. Customizing Company Settings

With your company details in place, it's time to fine-tune QuickBooks so it works the way you work. These settings control how sales, expenses, and accounting behaviors function behind the scenes. A little setup here saves hours later.

1. Customizing Sales Settings

Sales settings control how invoices look, how customers pay you, and how products and services are tracked.

1. Access Sales Settings:
   » Click the Gear icon at the top-right of your dashboard.
   » Select Account and Settings, then navigate to the Sales tab.

Settings			
Company	Sales form content	Preferred invoice terms ⓘ	Net 30 ▾
Usage		Preferred delivery method ⓘ	None ▾
Accounting		Shipping ⓘ	◯
Sales		Custom fields	
Expenses		Go to Settings > Lists > Custom Fields to manage your custom fields.	
Time		Custom transaction numbers ⓘ	●
Advanced		Service date ⓘ	Service date is required when using revenue recognition.
		Discount ⓘ	◯
		Deposit ⓘ	◯
		Tags ⓘ	●
		Cancel Save	
	Invoice payments	Payment instructions	
		No custom payment instructions added	
	Products and services	Show Product/Service column on sales forms	On
		Show SKU column	Off
		Turn on price rules	Off
		Track quantity and price/rate	On
		Track inventory quantity on hand	On
		Inventory valuation method ⓘ	Select Method
		Track inventory for sales channels	Off
		Revenue recognition Learn more	On
	Progress Invoicing	Create multiple partial invoices from a single estimate	Off

2. Configure Sales Form Content: these options shape what appears on your invoices and sales forms.
   » Preferred invoice terms: Set your default terms (Net 15, Net 30, etc.).

Choose something realistic for your clients and stay consistent—this feeds directly into your Accounts Receivable aging reports.

» Custom Transaction Numbers: Turn this on if you want control over invoice numbering or already have an external tracking system.

» Service Date: If you invoice for time-based services, turning this on gives your clients more clarity—and saves you time answering date-related questions.

» Discount and Deposit Fields: Only enable these if you use them regularly. I generally recommend keeping them off unless they're part of your standard workflow. Too many unused fields clutter your sales forms.

» Tags: Enable this for additional reporting flexibility. You can tag sales by campaign, sales rep, or region.

3. Invoice Payments & Instructions: Use this area to tell customers how you prefer to be paid (ACH, check, etc.). Clear instructions reduce delays and back-and-forth emails. We'll handle the actual payment processing setup in a dedicated section later..

4. Products and Services Tracking: These are crucial if you sell multiple items or services.

» Show Product/Service column – On: Essential for itemized invoices.

» Track quantity and price/rate – On: A major time-saver. Prices auto-fill and reduce manual errors.

» Inventory tracking: Turn it on if you sell physical products. Only enable this if your product list is accurate—inventory is not something you want to "fix later."

» SKU column & price rules: Best left off for service businesses. Retail or inventory-heavy operations may benefit from enabling these later.

» Revenue recognition: Turn it on as it is helpful for accrual-based businesses or longer-term projects where income is earned over time.

5. Other Helpful Sales Features:

» Progress Invoicing: This is a lifesaver for project-based businesses. Turn it on if you invoice in phases or based on project milestones.

» Statements and Reminders: Enable Statements to show aging details, and use Reminders to automatically nudge clients before or after due dates. It's like having a virtual assistant on your side.

Tip: If you have a team handling billing, set up these fields with clarity in mind. The more standardized your forms and defaults, the fewer errors and follow-ups you'll face.

Reminders Set up invoice reminder emails

☑ Use greeting Dear ▾ [Full Name] ▾

Use standard message **Insert placeholder ▾**

Email subject line

Reminder: Your payment to EverBloom Services is due

Email message

We're sending a reminder to let you know that invoice [Invoice No.] has not
been paid. If you already paid this invoice or have any questions, let us know!

Have a great day!
EverBloom Services

☐ Email me a copy at

Cancel Save

6. Save Your Customizations:

» Review all changes carefully and click Done to confirm.

2. Tailoring Expense Settings

Getting your expense settings right from the start helps you track where your money goes and makes tax time a whole lot smoother.

1. Access Expense Settings:

» Within Account and Settings, click on the **Expenses** tab.

2. Set Up Bills and Expenses: This section offers options that, when set up correctly, can save you hours of cleanup down the line:

Bills and expenses

Show Items table on expense and purchase forms ⑦

Show Tags field on expense and purchase forms ⑦

Track expenses and items by customer ⑦

Make expenses and items billable ⑦

Default bill payment terms Enter Text ▾

Cancel Save

» Show Items table: Turn this on if you frequently purchase inventory or services that require itemized tracking. It helps immensely during audits or when reviewing vendor trends.

» Show Tags field: I recommend enabling this to add more context to your expenses. Use tags to group costs by department, event, or internal project—whatever helps your business analyze spending smarter.

» Track by customer: Essential if you do job costing or need to allocate expenses to specific clients. Even if you don't bill back expenses, this visibility adds depth to your financial reports.

» Make expenses billable: If you recharge clients for purchases made on their behalf (like contractors, consultants, or designers often do), toggle this on. Just make sure to consistently check your billable expense reports so nothing slips through the cracks.

» Set clear default bill payment terms: Under Default bill payment terms, define how long you typically have to pay vendors. Setting this now ensures consistency and helps QuickBooks flag overdue bills.

3. Refine Purchase Order Settings: If you use purchase orders, especially for inventory or service-heavy businesses, toggle this feature on. Then:

» Customize the PO layout with custom fields for vendor references, internal codes, or project names.

» Add a default message that appears on all POs (e.g., "Please include PO number on invoice").

Tips: Don't ignore this area, even if you don't use POs regularly now. As your business scales, having these controls in place gives your operations structure and saves you from backtracking later.

4. Finalize Expense Settings:

» Click Save after each section to make sure your preferences are recorded.

3. Adjusting Advanced Company Settings

When it comes to managing your books with precision, the Advanced section in QuickBooks Online is where the magic happens. This is where you lay the groundwork for how your accounting system thinks, tracks, and behaves. Let's walk through the most important settings you should review and tailor to your business.

1. Go to Advanced Settings:

» Still within Account and Settings, select the Advanced tab.

2. Accounting Method & Fiscal Year

» Set your accounting method (cash or accrual) based on how you file taxes. Most small businesses use cash basis, but if you invoice customers and record income when it's earned, accrual might be the better fit. Also, define your fiscal year start month—typically January unless your business operates on a different annual cycle.

Tip: Always double-check this with your accountant or tax advisor before finalizing, as it impacts how your financials are reported.

Accounting	First month of fiscal year ⑦	January ▾
	First month of income tax year	Same as fiscal year ▾
	Accounting method ⑦	Accrual ▾
	Close the books ⑦	⬤

Cancel Save

3. Chart of Accounts
  » You can toggle the use of account numbers—highly recommended for larger or growing businesses for cleaner reports and easier classification.

4. Automation

Automation

  » You'll see options to pre-fill forms, and auto-invoice unbilled activity. While automation can save time, be cautious—

Pre-fill forms with previously entered content ⑦ ⬤
Automatically invoice unbilled activity ⑦ ⬤
Automatically apply bill payments ⑦ ⬤

especially with auto-invoices. It's better to stay hands-on until your workflow is fully refined.

Tip: Start with pre-filling enabled, but manually review automated actions until you're confident with the setup.

5. Review Carefully and Save:
  » Ensure all advanced settings align with your needs and click Save.

III. Connecting Bank and Credit Card Accounts

Connecting your bank and credit card accounts to QuickBooks Online is one of the most impactful setup steps you can take. Once connected, QuickBooks automatically brings in your transactions, helping you reduce manual data entry, stay current on your finances, and build reliable reports.

1. Accessing Bank Transactions

To get started:

1. From the left-hand navigation menu, click Accounting.
2. Select Bank transactions.

This takes you to the Bank Transactions dashboard, where QuickBooks guides you through automating your income and expense tracking. You'll see two primary options:

- Connect account (recommended)
- Upload transactions (manual alternative)

2. Linking Bank and Credit Card Accounts

Automatic bank feeds are the preferred method because they keep your books continuously updated.

1. Start the Connection:

   » On the Bank Transactions page, click the green Connect account button. QuickBooks will open the Connect an account window..

2. Find Your Financial Institution

   » Use the search bar to look up your bank or credit card provider by name or sign-in URL.

   » You may also see suggested banks based on popularity or past connections. If your bank appears in the list, select it to continue..

Let's find your account

Look up your provider by name or browse some of our suggestions.

Q Search by name or sign-in URL

Joint Stock Commerci...	Prescott State Bank
ModernAdvisor	Elite Client Account
M.E.S.A. Money Credit...	First Choice Communit...
Tata Cards (India) -...	Highlands Independen...

Show more

3. Sign In to Your Bank:

» Enter your online banking username and password.

» Complete any required security steps (such as verification codes or approval prompts).

» Some banks will also ask you to grant permission for QuickBooks to access your data. This is normal and required for the connection.

4. Choose Accounts to Connect

» Once signed in, QuickBooks will display a list of available accounts, such as: Checking accounts, Savings accounts or Credit cards.

» Select the account you want to connect and confirm or assign the correct QuickBooks account type.

Be intentional here—connecting unused or personal accounts can create unnecessary cleanup later.

5. Select the Download Start Date:

» Select how far back you'd like to import transactions.

Which accounts do you want to connect?

Choose account type

| ■■■■■■■■ail. | Cash and cash equivale ∨ | ∨ |

Balance: $80.66

We will pull transactions from the selected accounts from 12/17/2025. Or you can select a different date to pull transactions from. Some bank limitations may apply.

Today (2025-12-17) ∨

6. Click 'Connect':

» QuickBooks will begin importing transactions. You'll see a progress screen indicating money-in and money-out transactions being brought in.

3. Importing Bank Transactions Manually

If your bank isn't supported, or you need to backfill older data, you can upload manually.

1. Export your data in a supported format: CSV, QFX, OFX, TXT or QBO.

2. Upload to QuickBooks:

» Go to Accounting > Bank transactions, click the dropdown beside Link Account, and choose Upload from File.

» Select the account for the bank file then click Continue.

3. Map Your Fields:

> » QuickBooks will prompt you to match your file's columns with its data fields (Date, Description, Amount, etc.).

Step 1: Tell us about the format of your data

Is the first row in your file a header?

| Yes | ∨ |

How many columns show amounts?

| One column | ∨ |

What's the date format used in your file?

| MM/dd/yyyy | ∨ |

Step 2: Select the fields that correspond to your file

QuickBooks fields	Columns from your file
Date	Column 2: Posting D... ∨
Description	Column 3: Transacti... ∨
Amount	Column 4: Transacti... ∨
Check number (optional)	Select a check num... ∨

| Back | | Continue |

4. Verify and Import Your Transactions:

> » Verify how you want to import the positive and negative numbers (keep as-is or reverse all values).
> » Select the transactions you want to import.

Tip: Sometimes even with linking bank accounts, QuickBooks might miss some transactions. This is how you can select and import the missing ones.

5. Import and Review:

> » Once uploaded, the transactions will appear under the For Review tab, ready to be categorized.

4. Adding and Categorizing Transactions

All imported or synced transactions land in the Pending tab. Here's how to handle them:

1. Click a transaction to expand it.
2. Assign the right Category (e.g., Meals, Office Supplies, Sales Income).
3. Add a Vendor/Customer for better reporting and audit trail.
4. Use the Memo field to describe the transaction clearly (e.g., "Coffee meeting with client" or "Client payment – wedding décor").
5. Click Post to record it.

QuickBooks learns from your actions, so repeated transactions will be automatically suggested for faster review.

5. Matching Transactions

When QuickBooks detects a transaction that matches an existing entry—like a recorded invoice payment—it will suggest a match:

1. Go to Bank Transactions > Pending tab.
2. Look for suggestions marked as Match or filter Suggested matches.
3. Confirm and click Match if the details align.
4. If needed, click Find Match to manually search and link the correct entry.

6. Setting Up Bank Rules

If you're spending time categorizing the same types of transactions over and over—think coffee shops, recurring software charges, or fuel stops—it's time to embrace one of QuickBooks Online's most powerful features: Bank Rules.

Bank rules let you automate how QBO categorizes transactions based on conditions you define.

1. Navigate to Accounting > Rules.
2. Click New Rule.
3. Give it a clear, descriptive name (e.g., "Client Coffee Meetings" or "Monthly Adobe Subscription").
4. Choose whether the rule applies to Money In or Money Out.
5. Set the conditions—usually using the bank detail text. For example: Bank text contains "TikTok".
6. Assign a category, payee, and tax code.
7. Click Save.

Create rule   ×

Rules only apply to unreviewed transactions.

What do you want to call this rule? *

| Social Media Expenses |

Apply this to transactions that are

| Money out ⌄ | in | All bank accounts ⌄ |

and include the following: | All ⌄ |

| Description ⌄ | Contains ⌄ | TikTok |

+ Add a condition

| Test rule |

Then Assign ⌄

Transaction type | Expense ⌄ |

Category | Advertising & marketin ⌄ |

+ Add a split

Payee | Sample Customer ⌄ |

Tags | Start typing to add a ta |

+ Assign more

| Cancel | | Save |

Tip: Start with rules for recurring, predictable expenses—subscriptions, utilities, tolls. You can also create split rules for complex transactions.

By setting up your bank and credit card feeds properly, you streamline your workflow, reduce errors, and gain better insights into your cash flow. In the next section, we'll dive into customizing your Chart of Accounts to make your categories work harder for you.

IV. Customizing and Managing Your Chart of Accounts

Our next step is to customize and manage your Chart of Accounts, an essential element for maintaining clear and accurate financial records. Think of the Chart of Accounts as an organized system categorizing each business transaction, making it easy to track and analyze your finances effectively.

1. Understanding the Chart of Accounts Structure

The Chart of Accounts (COA) is essentially a list of all the financial accounts in your business. QuickBooks uses these accounts to organize your transactions into clear, insightful reports. Here's how your Chart of Accounts is typically structured:

- Assets: What your business owns (cash, inventory, equipment).
- Liabilities: What your business owes (loans, credit cards).
- Equity: Your ownership interest (owner's investments, retained earnings).
- Income: Revenue generated from sales and services.
- Expenses: Costs incurred in running your business (rent, utilities).

QuickBooks provides a default Chart of Accounts based on your industry type, but customizing it will better reflect your unique business structure and needs.

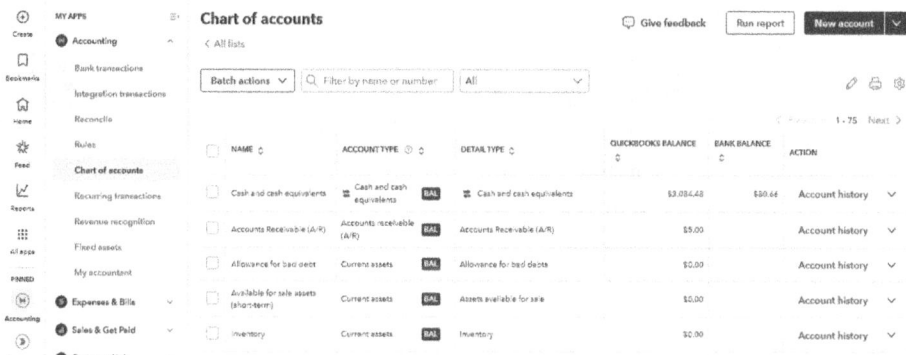

2. Understanding Account Type and Detail Type

To effectively use QuickBooks' Chart of Accounts, it's important to understand two key classifications: Account Type and Detail Type.

- Account Type: This broad category defines the general nature of each account, such as assets, liabilities, equity, income, and expenses. Account types help QuickBooks properly structure your financial reports and maintain consistency.

- Detail Type: This classification provides more specificity within each Account Type. QuickBooks uses Detail Types to offer guidance on common account usages and to further organize your financial information clearly. Selecting accurate Detail Types enhances reporting accuracy and clarity.

For example, under the Account Type "Assets," Detail Types might include bank accounts, accounts receivable, inventory, and fixed assets. Understanding and correctly assigning both Account and Detail Types ensures your financial records are precise and meaningful.

3. Creating and Customizing Accounts

Let's walk through the steps:

1. Navigate to Your COA:

    » Go to Accounting, then Charts of accounts.

2. Add a New Account:

    » Click New account.

    » Choose the account type (Asset, Liability, Equity, Income, Expense) from the dropdown menu.

3. Detail the Account:

    » Enter the account name clearly (like "Office Supplies" or "Sales Revenue").

    » Optionally, add a description to clarify the purpose of the account.

4. Set Additional Details:

    » Choose a sub-account if needed.

    » Click Save and Close once you're done.

New account   ×

Account name*

Event Planning Revenue

Account type*   ⓘ   Detail type*

Income   ∨   Sales of Product Income   ∨

☐ Make this a subaccount

Description

Profit & Loss   NEW ACCOUNT PREVIEW
Active accounts as of 04/02/2025

Billable Expense Income

Discounts given

Event Planning Revenue

Refunds to customers

Sales

Sales of Product Income

Services

Uncategorized Income

ⓧ Video tutorials   Cancel   Save   ∨

Don't be shy about creating new accounts—you can always edit or merge them later if needed.

4. Organizing Accounts for Efficient Bookkeeping

Keeping your Chart of Accounts tidy makes managing your finances quicker and easier. Here's how to organize your accounts efficiently:

- Use Sub-Accounts: Group related accounts under a primary account. For example, create sub-accounts for utilities (electricity, water, internet) under a main "Utilities" account.

- Be specific, but not overly detailed: Create specific accounts that are meaningful, but avoid unnecessary complexity. Your goal is clarity, not clutter.

- Review regularly: Periodically review your Chart of Accounts. Remove redundant or unused accounts to keep your reports streamlined.

By customizing and organizing your Chart of Accounts thoughtfully, you're setting yourself up for smooth, stress-free bookkeeping.

V. Importing, Editing, and Merging Accounts

Now that you've established your Chart of Accounts, let's dive into efficiently managing them. Whether importing accounts in bulk, updating account information, or streamlining duplicate accounts, QuickBooks Online makes these tasks simple and stress-free.

1. Importing Accounts from Excel or CSV Files

If you already have a list of accounts from another system or spreadsheet, you don't need to enter them manually—QuickBooks makes importing them a breeze:

1. Prepare Your File:

   » Organize your account data clearly in an Excel or CSV file.

   » Your file should include columns for Account Name, Account Type, Detail Type, and Description.

2. Start the Import Process:

   » Go to Chart of accounts. Click the dropdown next to New account and choose Import.

3. Upload Your File:

» Click Browse to locate your prepared Excel or CSV file and select it.

» Click Next to continue.

4. Map Your Fields:

» Match your file's columns to QuickBooks fields: Account Name, Type, Detail Type, Account number.

» Double-check your mappings carefully, then click Next.

5. Review and Complete:

» Review the preview QuickBooks provides to ensure accuracy. If you did not map your file's fields to all QuickBooks' required fields, you will have to manually review and map in this step.

» Click Import to finish the process.

2. Editing Existing Accounts

Keeping your Chart of Accounts up-to-date is vital for clear financial reporting. QuickBooks makes editing existing accounts quick and easy:

1. Locate the Account:

» Go to the Chart of Accounts.

» Scroll or search to find the account you need to edit.

2. Initiate Editing:

» Click the dropdown arrow next to the account and select Edit.

3. Update Account Details:

» Change the Account Name, Detail Type, or Description as needed.

» Ensure changes accurately reflect the current purpose of the account.

4. Save Your Changes:

» Click Save to apply the updates.

Regularly editing your accounts ensures your financial records remain clear, accurate, and effective.

3. Merging Duplicate or Redundant Accounts

Duplicate or redundant accounts can cause confusion and inaccuracies in your financial reports. Thankfully, QuickBooks allows you to merge accounts easily:

1. Identify the Accounts:

» Review your Chart of Accounts and pinpoint duplicate or unnecessary accounts.

2. Initiate the Merge:

» Decide which account you want to keep and note the exact name.

» Click the dropdown arrow next to the duplicate account you want to merge away and select Edit.

3. Rename to Merge:

» Change the duplicate account's name exactly to match the name of the account you're keeping.

» Click Save.

4. Confirm the Merge:

» QuickBooks will prompt you to confirm the merge. Click Yes to complete.

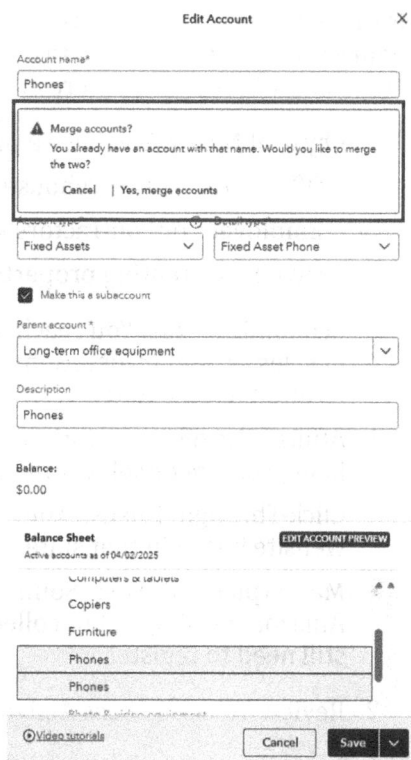

By merging duplicate accounts, your financial records stay tidy, streamlined, and easy to navigate.

VI. Understanding and Setting Up Sales Tax in QBO

It's time to tackle something every business owner must deal with: sales tax. It may sound intimidating at first, but QuickBooks Online makes it easier than ever to stay compliant and confident. In this section, we'll walk through how to understand your tax responsibilities and get everything set up correctly.

1. Identifying Tax Obligations

Sales tax nexus is one of those terms that sounds complicated—but it's essential for staying compliant with state tax laws. Simply put, nexus means a connection between your business and a state that requires you to collect and remit sales tax there. But how do you know if you have it?

Let's break down the key steps to determine whether your business has nexus, so you can charge sales tax correctly and avoid costly penalties down the road.

1. Understand What Creates Nexus:

Nexus is the connection between your business and a state or region that requires you to collect sales tax. Nexus can be created in a few ways—some physical, some economic. Here are the most common types:

- Physical Nexus: You have a physical presence in the state.
  » Office, store, or warehouse
  » Employees or contractors working in the state
  » Owning or renting property there
- Economic Nexus: You reach a certain sales threshold (usually $100,000 in sales or 200 transactions annually) even if you don't have a physical location in that state.
- Affiliate Nexus: You work with affiliates or third parties in the state who help promote or sell your products.
- Click-Through Nexus: Your sales are generated through links on a website based in that state.
- Marketplace Nexus: Some states require marketplaces (like Etsy, Amazon, or Shopify) to collect sales tax on your behalf—but you might still need to register.

2. Review Your Business Activities by State:

Start by asking yourself:

- Where are my customers located?
- Where do I ship physical goods?
- Do I have employees, reps, or contractors working remotely in any states?
- Do I participate in trade shows or do temporary business in other states?

- Do I store inventory in fulfillment centers (like Amazon FBA)?

Make a list of all the states where you have any business activity.

3. Check State-Specific Nexus Rules:

Every state sets its own rules for what creates nexus—especially for economic nexus. Here's how to check:

- Visit the State's Department of Revenue Website: Most have a section for "Remote Seller Guidelines" or "Sales Tax Nexus."
- Look for Thresholds: Economic nexus usually kicks in when your sales exceed $100,000 or 200 transactions annually in that state—but not always. Some states have higher or lower thresholds
- Determine If Marketplace Sales Count: Some states exclude sales made through marketplaces (e.g., Amazon), while others include them toward your nexus threshold.

4. Monitor Sales Regularly:

Even if you don't have nexus now, you might in the future. That's why it's critical to:

- Track sales by state inside QuickBooks or through your e-commerce platform.
- Set a monthly or quarterly reminder to review state-by-state totals.
- Pay attention to transaction count, not just revenue.

If you cross a threshold mid-year, most states expect you to register and begin collecting tax right away.

5. Register for Sales Tax Where Required:

If you determine that you do have nexus in a state:

- Register for a sales tax permit with that state's Department of Revenue.
- Start collecting and remitting sales tax based on that state's rules.
- Update your QuickBooks tax settings or app integrations accordingly.

Important: Never collect sales tax without registering first. It's illegal in most states and can trigger audits.

Understanding nexus isn't about playing defense—it's about being proactive. By following these steps, you'll know where you have obligations and how to stay compliant. To make it a bit easier, QuickBooks Online also offers a tool for you to determine if you need to charge sales tax just by simply answering a few questions. We will take a closer look at the next section.

2. Setting Up Sales Tax Rates

Once you know your obligations, it's time to bring sales tax into QuickBooks. Luckily, QuickBooks Online automates most of the work!

1. Enable Sales Tax in QuickBooks:

- Go to the All Apps in the left-hand navigation bar.
  - » Click Sales Tax, then Overview. Click on Set up sales tax to get started.

2. Enter Business Location:

- QuickBooks will ask for your primary business address. This helps determine which local and state taxes to apply.

3. Select Tax Filling Frequency:

- In the Sales Tax Center, you'll see a list of agencies you owe tax to.
  - » Set the correct filing frequency in QuickBooks based on your permit or agency requirements.

✓ Address	2 Tax agencies	3 Review and finish

You have to pay sales tax to these tax agencies

Based on your business address, you have to pay sales tax to these tax agencies. Tell us how often you file so we can track your deadlines and how much you owe. Your filing frequency is on your sales tax business registration.

TAX AGENCY	FILING FREQUENCY
Tennessee Department of Revenue › Contact info	Select frequency ⌄
	Annually
	Semi-Annually
	Quarterly
	Monthly

4. Confirm if you have registered for sales tax in other agency.

5. Review and Finish:

- Review the tax agencies QuickBooks sets up.
- Click Finish and turn on sales tax.

By understanding your tax obligations, setting up correct rates, and managing tax agencies confidently, you're taking a huge step toward building a business that's not only profitable but also compliant and professional.

Chapter 3: Managing Customers, Vendors, and Products

I. Setting Up and Organizing Your Customer List

One of the best things you can do for your books—especially if you invoice clients—is to take the time to properly set up your Customer List in QuickBooks Online. Whether you're offering services, products, or both, this list becomes your go-to tool for tracking who owes you money, managing communications, and running clean reports.

1. Understanding the Customer Hub

QuickBooks Online now organizes all customer-related activity inside the Customer Hub, making it easier to manage relationships, sales activity, and follow-ups from one central place. Instead of jumping between multiple menus, the Customer Hub brings everything tied to your customers into a single workflow.

You can access it by navigating to All apps → Customer Hub in the left-hand menu.

- Within the Customer Hub, you'll find several key sections:
- Overview: A high-level snapshot of customer activity, including recent transactions and key metrics.
- Leads: A place to track potential customers before they become paying clients. This is especially useful if you send estimates or proposals before invoicing.
- Customers: Your full customer list, where you manage customer profiles, view balances, create transactions, and review payment history.
- Estimates & Proposals: Tools for creating and tracking pre-sales documents, helping you move clients smoothly from inquiry to invoice.
- Reviews: If enabled, this section helps collect and manage customer feedback, supporting long-term relationship building.

The Customer Hub is designed to support the entire customer lifecycle—from lead to paid invoice—without leaving the same workspace, this means:

- Fewer clicks when following up on clients
- Better visibility into unpaid invoices and active projects
- A cleaner handoff from estimates to invoices to payments

Tip: Make it a habit to work directly from the Customer Hub when invoicing or reviewing receivables. It keeps your workflow consistent and reduces the chance of missing follow-ups or overdue balances.

2. Understanding the Customer area

When you click on All Apps > Customers Hub > Customers, you'll land in the main Customer page. From here, you can do the following efficiently:

- Search for Customers using the left-hand panel.

- Click into any customer to see their profile page, which includes:
  » A Summary panel showing open balances and overdue payments.

  » A transaction list showing invoices, payments, and more, filterable by type, date, or status.
  » Tabs for Statements, Recurring Transactions, Activity Feed, Tasks, Conversations, etc., giving you everything you need in one place.

On the right-hand side, QuickBooks offers quick actions like "Receive Payment" and "View/Edit", which allow you to act without navigating away from the customer view.

Tip: Regularly reviewing this page ensures you stay on top of aging receivables and quickly address payment issues. I recommend filtering and sorting by due date or amount to prioritize follow-ups. Whether you manage a handful of clients, this interface offers a scalable way to track your customer relationships and financials in one central hub.

Click to filter

3. Adding New Customers (Step-by-Step Guide)

Adding customers is straightforward and essential. Here's how:

1. Navigate to the Customers page.
2. Add Customer:
   » Click the green New Customer button.

3. Fill Out Customer Details:
   » Display Name: This is how the customer appears on invoices and reports.
   » Email Address: For sending invoices, reminders, and receipts.
   » Billing Address: This will be included on invoices and statements.
   » Phone & Other Contact Info: Helps if you need to follow up manually.
   » Payment Terms: Set defaults like "Net 30" or "Due on Receipt".
   » Notes or Tags (Optional): Handy for remembering special terms, project notes, or seasonal clients.

4. Save Your Entry:
   » Click Save. Your customer is now set up!

Repeat this process for each new customer you add.

4. Adding Multiple Customers at Once in QuickBooks Online

If you're migrating from another system or simply looking to set up multiple customers at once, QuickBooks Online's "Multiple Customers" option is a huge time-saver. Instead of entering customer details one by one, you can conveniently import or batch-enter numerous records all in one go. Here's how to efficiently tackle this:

1. Accessing the Multiple Customers Option:

   » Navigate to the Sales menu on the left hand sidebar.

   » Click on the Customers tab at the top.

   » From the New customer dropdown on the right, select Multiple customers.

2. Preparing Customer Data:

   » QuickBooks displays a spreadsheet-style interface where you can input key customer details, including some information such as Customer Name (mandatory), Parent Customer (for sub-customers), Company, Email and Contact Numbers, Payment Terms, etc.

   » You can directly type into these fields or copy-paste from an existing spreadsheet, streamlining your setup process significantly.

4. Complete the Import:

   » Once you confirm everything looks good, click Save.

   » QuickBooks instantly adds all these customers to your records, ready for invoicing, tracking, and reporting.

This method not only speeds up your workflow but ensures your customer database is comprehensive and accurate from the start—saving you valuable time for more strategic tasks.

5. Importing Customer Lists from Excel or CSV Files

If you have a long client list from another system, import it via CSV to save time—but double-check for duplicates and formatting issues before finalizing the upload.

1. Prepare Your File:

» Set up a simple spreadsheet with clear column headers like: Customer Name, Email, Phone Number, Billing Address, Notes, etc.

» Make sure each row is tidy—no merged cells or extra spaces.

	A	B	C	D	E	F
1	Customer Name	Customer Type	Contact Person	Email	Phone Number	Address
2	Portland Art Museum	Corporate	Emily Carter	ecarter@pam.org	(503) 555-1234	1219 SW Park Ave, Portland, OR 97205
3	Alder Creek Winery	Corporate	Mark Alder	malder@aldercreekwine.com	(503) 555-9876	3487 NE Alder Creek Ln, Newberg, OR 97132
4	Sarah and Thomas Williams	Wedding	Sarah Williams	sarah.williams@email.com	(503) 555-2345	4523 SE Clinton St, Portland, OR 97206
5	Benson Hotel	Corporate	Alex Martinez	alex.martinez@bensonhotel.com	(503) 555-6789	309 SW Broadway, Portland, OR 97205
6	Oregon Convention Center	Corporate	Lisa Ngo	lngo@oregoncc.org	(503) 555-4321	777 NE Martin Luther King Jr Blvd, Portland, OR 97232
7	The Wildwood Café	Recurring Client	Mia Daniels	mia@wildwoodcafe.com	(503) 555-2468	4701 SE Belmont St, Portland, OR 97215
8	Evergreen Golf Club	Private Event	Jonathan Wu	jon.wu@evergreengolf.com	(503) 555-1357	13450 NW Evergreen Pkwy, Beaverton, OR 97006
9	Rachel Baker	Wedding	Rachel Baker	rachelbaker@email.com	(503) 555-3579	2635 NE Wasco St, Portland, OR 97232

2. Start the Import:

» Go to All apps> Customers Hub > Customers, click the dropdown arrow beside New Customer, and select Import Customers.

3. Upload and Map Your File:

» Upload your file, then map each column in your spreadsheet to the correct QuickBooks fields. Take a moment here to make sure it all lines up—this step prevents cleanup later.

4. Review and Complete:

» Review the preview QuickBooks provides and click Import.

Import customers

UPLOAD

Map your fields to QuickBooks fields

QUICKBOOKS ONLINE FIELD	YOUR FIELD	
Name	Customer Name	✓
Company	No Match	
Email	Email	✓
Phone	Phone Number	✓
Mobile	No Match	
Fax	No Match	
Website	No Match	
Street	Address	✓
City	No Match	
Province/Region/State	No Match	
ZIP code	No Match	
Country	No Match	
Opening Balance	No Match	
Opening Balance Date	No Match	

Tip: Before importing, scan for duplicate names, inconsistent formatting (e.g., "John Doe" vs "Doe, John"), or missing email addresses. A clean list means smoother invoicing and more accurate reports from day one.

6. Categorizing and Editing Customers

QuickBooks lets you go beyond a flat list—you can categorize customers for better segmentation and smarter reporting using Customer Types.

You can create custom customer types that reflect your business model. If you're unsure where to start, I recommend grouping clients based on how they interact with your business. Common examples include: Retail, Wholesale, Event Clients, or Subscription Clients.

To categorize:

1. Click Customer Hub > Customers. Choose a customer and click Edit.

2. Scroll to Additional Info and select customer type.
3. Click Save to confirm.

Set up customer types before you import or enter new clients. That way, you can track sales performance by group and tailor your messaging.

7. Merging Duplicate Customer

Over time, duplicate customer records can sneak into your system—especially after imports or manual entry. Merging customers helps keep your books clean and ensures invoices, payments, and reports stay accurate.

How to Merge Customers

1. Go to All apps > Customers Hub > Customers.
2. Click the customer record you want to keep. Select Edit, then choose Merge contacts.
3. In the Merge contacts window:
   » Choose the duplicate customer you want to merge from.
   » Confirm the customer you are merging into.
4. Click Merge contacts to finalize.

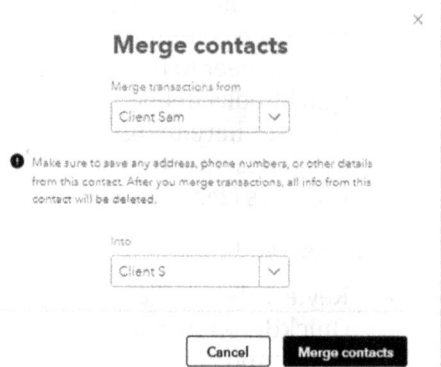

QuickBooks will move all transactions from the duplicate customer into the remaining profile and remove the extra record.

Note:

- Merges cannot be undone. Once completed, there's no rollback.
- All transactions transfer to the surviving customer record.
- Contact details do not merge automatically. Make sure you save any important email addresses, phone numbers, or notes before confirming.

If you're unsure, pause and review both customer profiles first. A careful merge now prevents reporting issues and confusion later—especially when reviewing sales by customer or A/R aging reports.

II. Managing Vendor Information Efficiently

1. Understanding the Vendor List Structure

Your vendor list in QuickBooks Online serves as a comprehensive directory for every supplier or contractor your business interacts with. When you navigate to Expenses > Vendors, you'll see a well-organized dashboard that gives you immediate insights into your payables:

- At the top, QuickBooks summarizes unbilled, unpaid, and paid activity—so you always know where your business stands.

- Below that, you'll find a searchable, sortable vendor list, showing key fields like:
  » Vendor Name and Company Name
  » Email and Phone
  » Open Balances
  » 1099 Tracking Status
  » Quick Action

You can customize with optional columns like Attachments, Address, or to Include Inactive Vendors—just click the gear icon in the top right to adjust your view. QuickBooks even gives you a shortcut to Create Bill directly from this list, streamlining your workflow without having to dig into submenus.

2. Adding New Vendors Manually

Adding vendors properly from the start saves time later—and keeps your books cleaner and more organized. Here's how you do it:

1. Access the Vendor List:
   » Select Expenses from the left-hand menu. Click Vendors.

2. Add a Vendor: Click on the green New Ve

3. Fill in Vendor Details:

  » Enter essential details including name, address, phone number, email, payment terms, and tax ID if available.

  » Attach documents or add notes for additional context.

4. Save the Vendor: Click Save to add the vendor to your list.

Tip: If you plan to track 1099 contractors, make sure to check the box for tracking payments for 1099 while setting them up. It's much easier than updating this later during tax season.

3. Adding Multiple Vendors

When managing a growing business, you're likely juggling numerous suppliers, contractors, or service providers. QuickBooks Online simplifies vendor management by allowing you to add multiple vendors simultaneously—saving you valuable time and minimizing errors.

Here's how you can quickly add multiple vendors:

1. Navigate to the Vendors Section:

  » Click Expenses from the left-hand menu, then select the Vendors tab.

2. Select Multiple Vendors:

  » Click the green New Vendor button on the right side of the screen.

  » Choose Multiple vendors from the dropdown menu.

3. Use the Batch Transactions Tool:

  » You'll see a spreadsheet-style interface allowing you to input vendor details in bulk.

  » Easily enter vendor names, company information, emails, phone numbers, addresses, and other essential details directly into the provided fields.

4. Customize Your Columns (Optional):

» Click Customize columns to rearrange, add, or remove fields according to your preference, ensuring the spreadsheet matches your existing records or workflow.

5. Review and Save:

» Double-check your entries for accuracy. Once you're satisfied, click Save to create these vendors all at once in your QuickBooks database.

By taking advantage of the multiple-vendor entry tool, you streamline your bookkeeping, reduce manual data entry, and keep your vendor management organized and accurate—giving you more time to focus on running your business smoothly.

4. Importing Vendor Information

If you already have a list of vendors from another system or spreadsheet, importing them into QuickBooks Online can save you serious time—especially when setting up a new file. Here's how to do it:

1. Prepare Your File First: Set up your vendor list in Excel or CSV format. Use clean headers like: Vendor Name, Company Name, Email, Phone Number, Billing Address, Tax ID (if applicable)

Tip: Double-check for duplicates or formatting issues before uploading. Cleaning the data before import always saves a headache later.

	A	B	C	D	E
1	Vendor Name	Company Name	Email	Phone Number	Billing Address
2	Laura Nichols	Nichols Office Supplies	laura@nicholsoffice.com	(555) 123-4567	100 Maple Street, Seattle, WA 98101
3	Kevin Brown	Brown Landscaping Co.	kevin@brownlandscaping.com	(555) 987-6543	230 Spruce Ave, Portland, OR 97201
4	Michelle Turner	Turner Design Studio	michelle@turnerstudio.com	(555) 246-8101	412 Oak Road, San Francisco, CA 94103
5	Alejandro Rivera	Rivera HVAC Services	alejandro@riverahvac.com	(555) 135-7913	789 Pine Blvd, Los Angeles, CA 90001

2. Start the Import

» Go to Expenses > Vendors.

» Click the gear icon in the top right corner of the vendor table and select Import Vendors.

» Upload your CSV or Excel file.

3. Map Your Fields: QuickBooks will ask you to match your file's columns to QuickBooks fields. Confirm that each column (like "Phone Number") matches the right destination.

4. Review and Complete: After

Import vendors

UPLOAD

Map your fields to QuickBooks fields

QUICKBOOKS ONLINE FIELD	YOUR FIELD	
Name	Vendor Name	✓
Company	Company Name	✓
Email	Email	✓
Phone	Phone Number	✓
Mobile	No Match	
Fax	No Match	
Website	No Match	
Street	Billing Address	✓
City	No Match	
Province/Region/State	No Match	

mapping, review the import preview carefully. If everything looks good, click Import to finish.

5. Editing Existing Vendor Profiles

Regularly updating vendor details keeps your information precise and up-to-date:

1. Locate Your Vendor:
   » Click Expenses > Vendors.
   » Find and select the vendor to edit.

2. Make Necessary Edits:
   » Click Edit to update the vendor's contact details, payment terms, or other information.

3. Save Changes:
   » Review your edits, then click Save.

Accurate vendor profiles facilitate smooth business transactions and communication.

6. Merging Vendor Information

Simplify managing your vendor information by merging duplicates:

1. Clearly identify any duplicates.
2. Edit the duplicate vendor's name to exactly match the name of the vendor profile you wish to keep.
3. QuickBooks will prompt you to confirm the merge—click Yes.

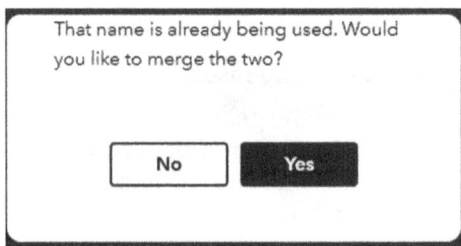

That name is already being used. Would you like to merge the two?

No   Yes

Keeping your vendor records organized enables smoother daily operations and financial management. You're now fully equipped to effectively manage vendor information—another impressive step toward mastering QuickBooks!

III. Managing Products and Services for Better Sales and Inventory Tracking

Accurate product and service management in QuickBooks Online significantly boosts your sales tracking, inventory control, and overall business efficiency.

1. Understanding Products and Services in QuickBooks

The Products and Services list in QuickBooks isn't just a catalog—it's the financial backbone of your sales and purchasing workflows. It connects what you sell or buy to the right income and expense accounts, keeps your invoicing accurate, and helps you understand your business performance in real time.

Here's what you'll see—and what it all means:

NAME	QTY ON HAND	QTY ON PO	QTY ON SO	AVAIL QTY	CATEGORY	SKU	TYPE	PRICE	COST	ACTION
Boutonniere & Corsage (Set)		0	0		Custom Products	CP-BOCO	Service	0	0	Edit | ∨
Customized Bridal Bouquet		0	0		Custom Products	CP-BRBQ	Service	0	0	Edit | ∨
Decorative Vase	50	0	0	50	Floral Supplies	FS-VASE01	Inventory	0	0	Edit | ∨
Delivery & Setup		0	0		Event Services	ES-DELIV	Service	0	0	Edit | ∨

Columns That Matter:

- Name – This is the item's name as it appears on invoices, estimates, and sales forms. Keep it client-friendly and specific (e.g., "Event Planning – Mini Package" instead of just "Service").
- Qty on Hand – Only shown for inventory items. QuickBooks tracks this in real time so you never oversell or run short.
- Category – Helps you group items for better reporting. For example, group all decor services under "Event Planning."
- SKU – Optional but helpful for internal tracking or syncing with inventory systems.
- Type – Indicates whether it's a Service, Inventory item, Non-inventory item, or Bundle. Each has its own accounting behavior.
- Price – The rate you charge customers. Set it once, and it auto-fills on sales forms.
- Cost – If you also purchase the item, this field reflects the expense side.
- Action – Quick access to Edit, Make inactive, or run respective reports.

Efficiently managing your products and services enhances your decision-making and profitability.

2. Adding New Products and Services

Whether you're selling handcrafted goods, professional services, or bundled packages, setting up your product and service list in QuickBooks Online is essential for clean, accurate books and efficient invoicing. Done right, it makes everything—from revenue tracking to tax prep—simpler and smarter.

Step-by-Step Setup:

1. Navigate to Sales & Get Paid > Products & Services: Click "Create items" to begin setting up.

2. Choose the Right Item Type: You'll see four options in the Item type dropdown:

   » Service – For billable time or project-based work (e.g., event planning, consulting).

   » Inventory item – For goods you buy and sell and want to track quantities for.

   » Non-inventory item – For physical items you don't track (like office supplies or materials used on the spot).

   » Bundle – A group of products/services sold together (perfect for packages or kits).

Choose the correct type from the start. Switching item types later is limited—especially for inventory—so get it right upfront. The interface slightly varies between different item type.

3. Fill Out Basic Information

   » Name: Make it short but descriptive. This appears on invoices.

   » SKU/Image: Optional, but useful for inventory or visual catalogs.

   » Category: Use categories to group similar items for better reporting.

4. Complete the Sales Section

   » Check "I sell this service to my customers" if prompted.

   » Add a clear description that shows on sales forms.

   » Set your rate and assign an appropriate income

account (e.g., Services Income, Product Sales).

Tip: Avoid lumping everything into "Sales." Break out income by line of business or product type for more meaningful insights in your Profit & Loss reports.

5. Optional: Complete the Purchasing Section: If you also buy this item from vendors, check the box and fill in the cost, purchase description, and expense account (e.g., Cost of Goods Sold or Subcontractor expenses).

6. Save Your Item: When finished, click Save and close or Save and new to continue adding items.

3. Importing Products and Services into QuickBooks Online

When you have numerous products or services to add to QuickBooks, importing them in bulk from Excel or CSV files can significantly streamline your setup. Here's how you can effectively import these items:

Using Spreadsheet Sync (Excel):

This method is ideal if you're comfortable working directly in Excel and prefer seamless integration between Excel and QuickBooks:

1. Select Settings, then select Import Data.

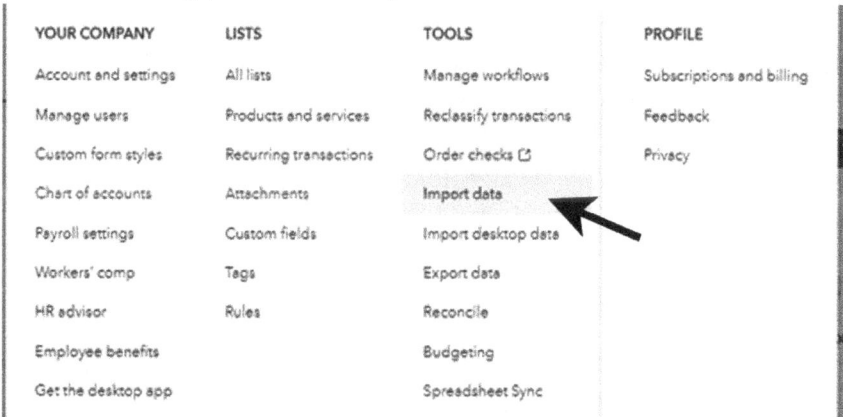

YOUR COMPANY	LISTS	TOOLS	PROFILE
Account and settings	All lists	Manage workflows	Subscriptions and billing
Manage users	Products and services	Reclassify transactions	Feedback
Custom form styles	Recurring transactions	Order checks ☐	Privacy
Chart of accounts	Attachments	Import data	
Payroll settings	Custom fields	Import desktop data	
Workers' comp	Tags	Export data	
HR advisor	Rules	Reconcile	
Employee benefits		Budgeting	
Get the desktop app		Spreadsheet Sync	

2. Select the Products and Services in the dropdown menu. Then click Import.

3. Choose Import from Excel using Spreadsheet Sync.

4. Install the Spreadsheet Sync add-in for Excel, authorize it, and log in with your QuickBooks account.

What do you want to import?

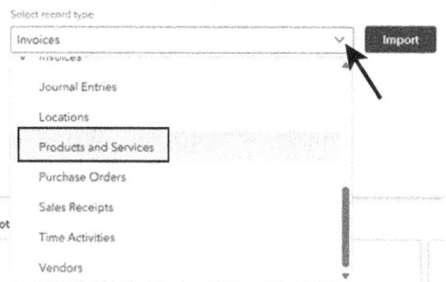

Select record type

Invoices

- Invoices
- Journal Entries
- Locations
- Products and Services
- Purchase Orders
- Sales Receipts
- Time Activities
- Vendors

Import

5. Click the Spreadsheet Sync add-in in Exel, then select Create or edit records.

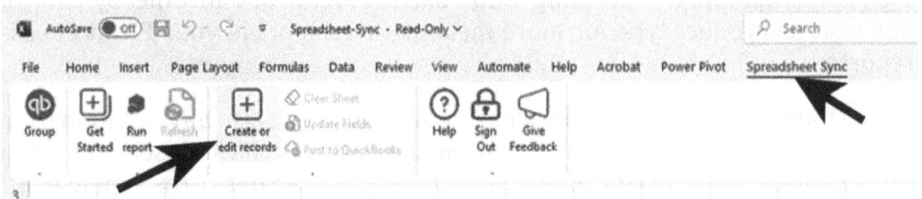

6. Select Inventory Item as record type, choose between adding new records or editing records and click Get Template.

7. Fill in the template directly in Excel.

8. Then sync the data instantly to QuickBooks.

Batch Import (CSV):

Alternatively, instead of messing with add-in with Excel, you can directly import a CSV file to QuickBooks:

1. Follow step 1 and step 2 above, then choose Use QuickBooks Batch transactions or navigate to Products & Services, click the dropdown next to New, then choose Batch import.

2. Click Import CSV, upload your prepared file.

3. Map the columns in your spreadsheet to QuickBooks fields, such as Product Name, SKU, Sales Price, Income Account, and Quantity on Hand.

4. Review the mapped data carefully before clicking Save to finalize the import.

Map your column headings

Review and map the column headers in your CSV file with the QuickBooks fields. Required fields are marked an asterisk (*).

QUICKBOOKS FIELDS	CSV COLUMN HEADERS
*Product/service name	Name
Category	Category
*Item type	Type
SKU	SKU

4. Importing through Sales Channels:

If your business utilizes online marketplaces such as Amazon, eBay, Etsy, or Shopify, QuickBooks provides direct integration to streamline importing product data.

Simply choose Import from sales channel from the New dropdown in the Products & Services tab and connect the relevant marketplace.

Recommendation: Always review and validate imported data to ensure accuracy. Properly organized product and service listings in QuickBooks help optimize your workflow, improve inventory management, and enhance financial reporting accuracy.

5. Editing Existing Products and Services

Keeping your product and service details accurate is crucial. Here's how to update them:

1. Access the Products and Services List:
   » Go to Sales & Get Paid > Products & services.

2. Edit Item Details:
   » Locate and click the item to update.
   » Click Edit, make your changes, and review carefully.

NAME	QTY ON HAND	QTY ON PO	QTY ON SO	AVAIL QTY	CATEGORY	SKU	TYPE	PRICE	COST	ACTION
Boutonniere & Corsage (Set)		0	0	0	Custom Products	CP-BOCO	Service	0	0	Edit ∨

3. Save Changes:

» Click Save and Close to confirm updates.

Managing your products and services effectively with QuickBooks ensures your business stays profitable, organized, and customer-ready.

CHAPTER 4: MASTERING EVERYDAY TRANSACTIONS

I. Creating and Sending Professional Invoices

QuickBooks Online makes invoicing easy, professional, and streamlined, enhancing your cash flow and customer relationships.

1. Designing and Customizing Invoice Templates

Invoices represent your brand, so let's ensure they look professional and appealing:

1. Navigate to Invoice Customization:
   » Click the Gear icon at the top-right corner.
   » Select Custom Form Styles.

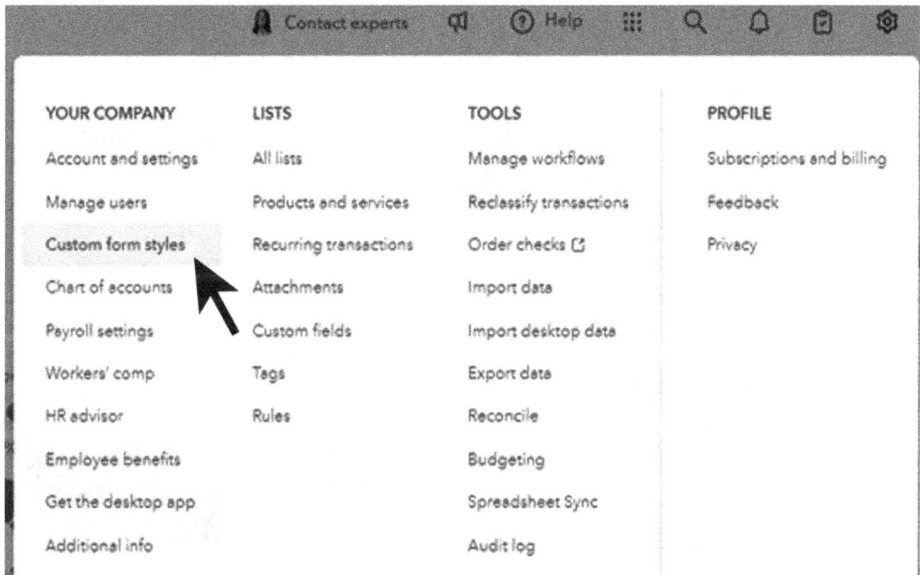

2. Create or Edit Templates:
   » Click New Style or select an existing template to modify.
   » Choose Invoice from the options.

3. Personalize Your Invoice:
   » Select your logo and preferred colors to reflect your brand identity.
   » Choose fonts and layout to enhance readability.
   » Define the content you want displayed, such as invoice numbers,

payment terms, and custom messages.

Design	Content	Emails

My INVOICE Template - 4-10 (30

Change up the template

EverBloom
SERVICES

Show logo

Try other colors

Ff Select a different font

Edit print settings

EverBloom Services

INVOICE

BILL TO				INVOICE	12345
Smith Co.				DATE	01/12/2016
123 Main Street				TERMS	Net 30
City, CA 12345				DUE DATE	02/12/2016

DATE	ACTIVITY	DESCRIPTION	QTY	RATE	AMOUNT
12/01/2016	Item name	Description of the item	2	$225.00	$450.00
01/12/2016	Item name	Description of the item	1	$225.00	$225.00

	SUBTOTAL	$675.00
	DISCOUNT 2%	-$13.50
	TOTAL	$661.50
	BALANCE DUE	**$675.00**

Page 1 of 1

4. Preview and Save:

» Preview your customized invoice. Click Save to apply the changes.

» Make your customized template as default.

Your invoices now reflect your unique brand and professionalism.

EverBloom Services

Knoxville,
USA

BILL TO
Smith Co.
123 Main Street
City, CA 12345

| Invoice 12345 |
| DATE: 01/12/2016   TERMS: Net 30 |
| DUE DATE: 02/12/2016 |

DATE	ACTIVITY	DESCRIPTION	QTY	RATE	AMOUNT
12/01/2016	Item name	Description of the item	2	225.00	450.00
01/12/2016	Item name	Description of the item	1	225.00	225.00

	SUBTOTAL	675.00
	DISCOUNT 2%	-13.50
	TOTAL	$675.00
	TOTAL DUE	$675.00

2. Creating Invoices Step-by-Step

Ready to create invoices effortlessly? Follow these straightforward steps:

1. Navigate to Invoicing:
   » In the top left sidebar, go to + Create > Invoices.

2. Select Your Customer:
   » Choose your customer from the drop-down list or add a new one on the fly.

3. Fill in Invoice Details:
   » Enter invoice date, payment terms, and due date.
   » Add products or services, descriptions, quantities, and rates.
   » QuickBooks automatically calculates totals and taxes.

4. Review and Save:
   » Review the information carefully.
   » Click Save or Review and send depending on your needs.

3. Sending, Printing, and Tracking Status of Invoices

After creating an invoice, QuickBooks offers simple tools to manage and track its status:

Sending Invoices:

- Choose Review and send to email the invoice directly from QuickBooks. Customize your email message if needed, and click Send invoice.
- Send Reminder to remind customers of unpaid invoices.

Tracking Invoice Status:

- Navigate to Sales & Get Paid > Invoices.
- Easily track invoice statuses—sent, viewed, paid, or overdue.
- Send reminders for unpaid invoices directly from this screen.

$5,281.52 Unpaid Last 365 days   **$3,692.22 Paid** Last 30 days

$1,525.50   **$3,756.02**   **$2,062.52**   **$1,629.70**

Overdue   Not due yet   Not deposited   Deposited

Printing Invoices:

- Select the Print or download option at the bottom of your invoice creation screen. Or:

- Navigate to Sales & Get Paid > Invoices, then select Print option next to the invoice.

INVOICE

EverBloom Services

Knoxville,

!gmail.com

+1

EverBloom
SERVICES

Bill to
Alder Creek Winery
3487 NE Alder Creek Ln, Newberg, OR
97132

Invoice details
Invoice no.: 1004
Terms: Net 30
Invoice date: 04/10/2025
Due date: 05/10/2025

#	Product or service	Description	Qty	Rate	Amount
1.	Customized Bridal Bouquet	Bridal Bouquet	1	$80.00	$80.00

	Total	$80.00

Ways to pay

ePay VISA ⬤⬤ DISCOVER BANK

View and pay

With QuickBooks' efficient invoicing tools, managing your business cash flow becomes straightforward, professional, and hassle-free.

II. Creating and Sending Estimates in QuickBooks Online

Whether you're a floral designer quoting a custom event or a contractor outlining project costs, estimates help you set expectations upfront— before money changes hands. In QuickBooks Online, creating, managing, and converting estimates is simple and efficient. Let's walk through the full process.

1. Create and Customize an Estimate

Start by creating a professional-looking estimate tailored to your brand and your customer's needs.

1. From the left menu, click All Apps > Customer Hub > Estimate. Alternatively, in the top left sidebar, click + Create > Estimate.

2. Select the Customer from your list (or add a new one).

3. Enter the Estimate Date and Expiration Date, if applicable.

4. Add Products or Services:

   » Include quantity, rate, and any custom descriptions.

   » Double-check tax settings—make sure taxable items are flagged correctly.

Lewis & Clark College ⌄						
bsullivan@lclark.edu						
Cc/Bcc						
Bill to	**Location of Sale (hidden)**		Estimate no.	1001	Accepted by	
Lewis & Clark College 615 S Palatine Hill Rd, Portland, OR 97219	Knoxville.		Estimate date	04/14/2025	Accepted date	MM/DD/YYYY
			Expiration date	04/30/2025		
Edit Customer	Add shipping info					

Tags (hidden):   Manage tags

Start typing to add a tag

Product or service

#	Product/service	Description	Qty	Rate	Amount	Tax	
1	Floral Arrangements:Orchid ...		20	35	$700.00	☑	⋮

5. Customize the appearance:

   » Use the Customize and Design field to apply your preferred content and color scheme.

   » Add a personal message for clarity or warmth—especially helpful in service-based businesses.

Estimate 1001   ✕

Edit default settings

Pending ⌄

Customization	⌄
Discounts and Fees	⌄
Design	⌄
Scheduling	⌄
Customer reports	⌄

Pro Tip: Add your logo and payment terms to give your estimate a polished, trustworthy appearance. First impressions matter.

6. Save and Send the Estimate

Once you are done, click Save. To email the estimate to your customer, select Review and send. Edit the email message, if necessary, and select Send estimate.

2. Update Estimate Status

Tracking where each estimate stands helps you manage follow-ups and forecast income more accurately.

Estimate statuses include:

- Pending – Just created or sent
- Accepted – Customer has agreed to it
- Declined – Not approved by the customer

To update the status manually:

1. Go to Sales > Estimates.
2. Click the dropdown under the Action column then click Update Status.

	DATE	NO.	CUSTOMER	AMOUNT	STATUS ▲	ACTION ⚙
☐	4/14/25	1003	Rachel Baker	$655.50	✅ Accepted	View/Edit │ Convert to invoice │ ▼
☐	4/14/25	1002	Portland Art Museum	$327.75	Pending	View/Edit │ Send │ ▼
☐	4/14/25	1001	Lewis & Clark College	$764.75	Pending	

Mark accepted

View/Edit

Duplicate

Share estimate link

Print

Update Status

Copy to purchase order

Delete

View activity

First   Previous   1

3. Save the changes to keep your pipeline accurate.

Batch actions ⌄	Status	Date					Create estimate
	All ⌄	Last 12 months ⌄					

	DATE	NO.	CUSTOMER	AMOUNT	STATUS ▲	ACTION ⚙
☐	12/28/25	1001	Lewis & Clark College	$700.00	✅ Accepted	View/Edit │ Convert to invoice │ ▼
☐	12/28/25	1003	Lewis & Clark College	$1,000.00	Pending	View/Edit │ Send │ ▼
☐	11/30/25	1002	Client Sam	$600.00	⊗ Declined	View/Edit │ Print │ ▼

Reviewing estimate statuses regularly can help you follow up with leads, prioritize workload, and forecast cash flow.

3. Convert an Estimate to an Invoice

Once you complete the service or deliver products to your customer and your customer gives the green light, it's time to turn the estimate into invoice.

Here's how to convert:

1. Find the approved estimate and click Convert to invoice.
2. Choose whether to:
   » Invoice the full amount at once
   » Invoice a percentage of the estimate (great for deposits)
   » Invoice selected line items only (perfect for multi-stage jobs)

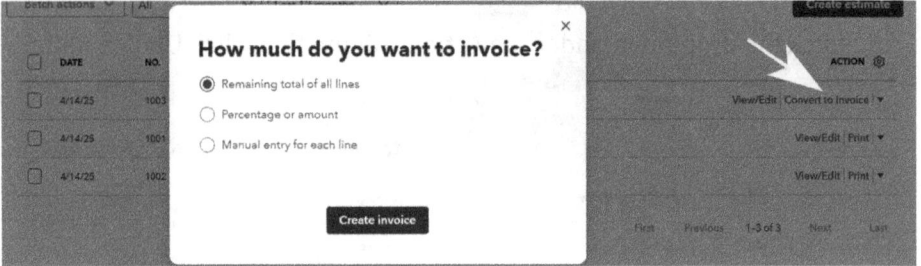

3. Review and customize the invoice as needed.
4. Click Review and Send to email the invoice, or Save and Close if you'll send it later.

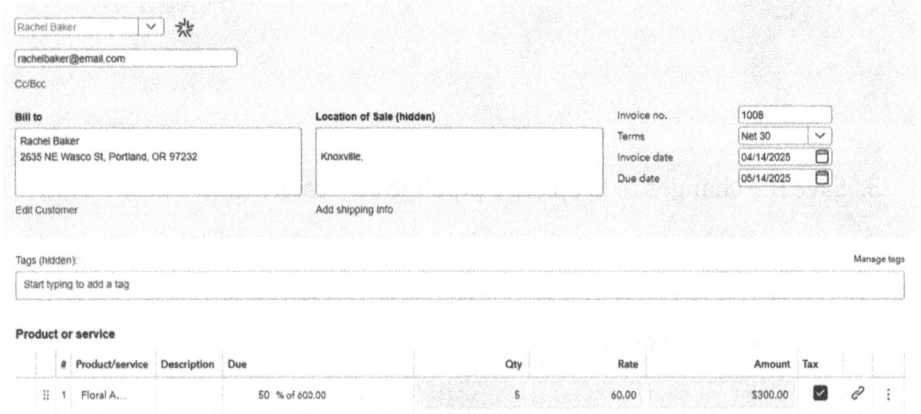

Important: The options in Step 3 only appear if you have turned on progress invoicing. To turn it on, go to the setting under Settings > Account and Settings > Sales > Progress Invoicing.

4. Delete Mistaken Estimates

Every business makes a few extra clicks now and then. Luckily, QuickBooks makes it easy to clean up. To delete an estimate:

1. Open the estimate you want to remove.

2. Click the dropdown next to More at the bottom.

3. Select Delete > confirm.

Tip: Only delete estimates if they were created by mistake. If a customer rejected the quote, it's better to update the status to Rejected to preserve the record for future reference.

III. Receiving and Recording Customer Payments

QuickBooks Online streamlines this process, helping you record and track payments efficiently, so you can spend less time on bookkeeping and more time growing your business.

1. Recording Payments from Customers

As soon as a payment arrives, promptly entering it into QuickBooks ensures your records remain accurate and up-to-date. Here's a quick step-by-step guide:

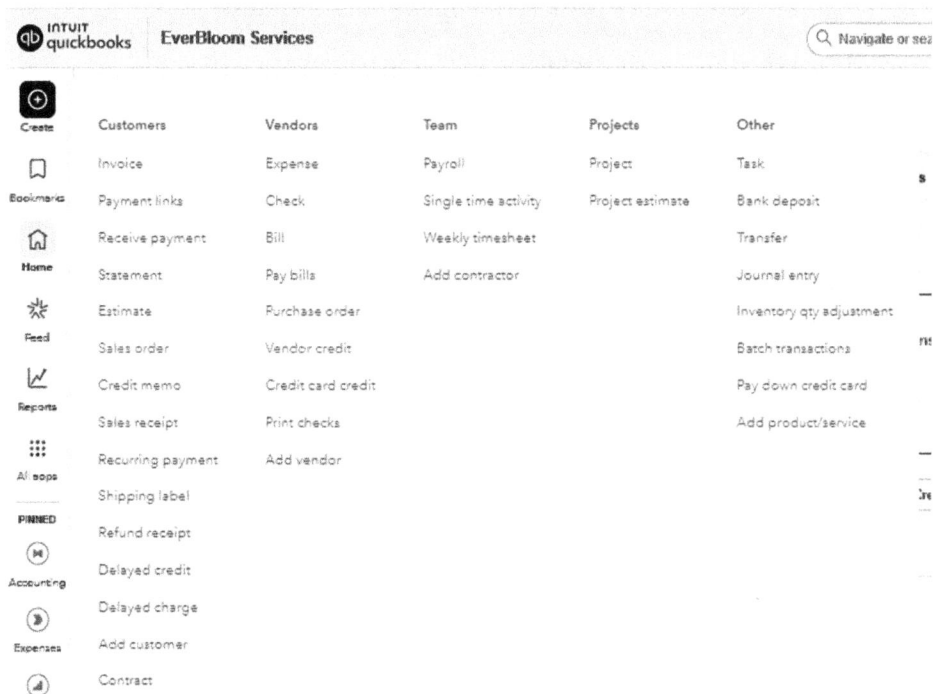

	Customers	Vendors	Team	Projects	Other
Create	Invoice	Expense	Payroll	Project	Task
Bookmarks	Payment links	Check	Single time activity	Project estimate	Bank deposit
Home	Receive payment	Bill	Weekly timesheet		Transfer
	Statement	Pay bills	Add contractor		Journal entry
Feed	Estimate	Purchase order			Inventory qty adjustment
	Sales order	Vendor credit			Batch transactions
Reports	Credit memo	Credit card credit			Pay down credit card
	Sales receipt	Print checks			Add product/service
AI bots	Recurring payment	Add vendor			
	Shipping label				
PINNED	Refund receipt				
Accounting	Delayed credit				
	Delayed charge				
Expenses	Add customer				
	Contract				

1. Navigate to Receive Payment:

   » Click + Create at the top-left corner of your QuickBooks dashboard, then select Receive Payment under the Customers category.

2. Select Customer and Enter Payment Details:

» Choose the correct customer from the drop-down menu. Or find the customer using invoice number.

» Input the payment date, exact payment amount, and payment method (e.g., cash, check, credit card, or bank transfer).

» Recommendation: Clearly specify the payment method. This helps greatly with future bank reconciliations and auditing.

3. Select the invoice that you are receiving payment for.

» If you are receiving partial payment for multiple invoices, QuickBooks allows you to enter manually how much you receive for each invoice.

» Without an invoice, QuickBooks Online gives you a few options to record the payment: sales receipt or credit to customers.

4. Deposit to the Appropriate Bank Account:

» Choose the correct deposit account. Typically, if payments will be grouped and deposited later, select Undeposited Funds. If the payment goes directly into your bank account, select that account.

Tip: Use Undeposited Funds to batch multiple payments into one deposit, mirroring the actual deposit made to the bank. This simplifies the reconciliation process considerably. We will take a detailed look at later section.

5. Review and Save:

» Always double-check payment details before finalizing. Once verified, click Save and Close.

Timely and accurate payment recording safeguards your financial clarity and improves cash flow visibility.

2. Handling Full and Partial Payments

Customers will occasionally submit partial payments, and QuickBooks handles these scenarios seamlessly:

- Full Payments: Simply record the full amount; QuickBooks automatically marks the invoice as paid, streamlining your accounts receivable process.

- Partial Payments: Enter the exact amount received. QuickBooks then calculates and tracks the outstanding balance automatically, making follow-up straightforward.

	DATE	NO.	CUSTOMER ▲	AMOUNT	STATUS		ACTION ⚙
☐	4/10/25	1004	Alder Creek Winery	$80.00	✓ Deposited		View/Edit | Print | ▾
☐	4/10/25	1006	Alder Creek Winery	$150.00	Partially paid $120.00 due		View/Edit | Receive payment | ▾

Recommendation: Regularly review open balances and promptly follow up with customers. QuickBooks reporting tools help you manage these outstanding receivables efficiently.

3. Matching Bank Transactions to Recorded Payments

To maintain organized and error-free bookkeeping, ensure all payments entered into QuickBooks match with actual bank transactions:

1. Go to Banking Transactions:

» Navigate to Banking from the left menu and select the account receiving payments.

2. Confirm QuickBooks Matches:

» QuickBooks automatically suggests matching transactions based on amounts and dates.

» Review these suggestions carefully, then confidently click Match.

| | 03/13/2025 | | 55 Twin Lane | 1 match found Payment 03/13/2025 $50.00 55 Twin Lane | | $50.00 | Match |

○ Categorize ● Match ○ Record as transfer   ✕

Suggested match: Also $50.00 and falls between 12/13/2024-4/2/2025.

Payment 03/13/2025 $50.00 55 Twin Lane

Not the right match? Find other matches

BANK DETAIL No description available from

(Find other matches) (Match)

3. **Manual Matching (If Required):**

Find other matches   ⑦ ✕

From	To	Filter by	Search
04/10/2024	05/10/2025	All ▼	Reference number, payee, or amount 🔍

Suggested matches 🔘

If none of these groups look right, turn off suggested matches to see the full list.

[3 Multiple ✓] [3 Multiple]

Select transaction to match

	DATE	TYPE	REF NUMBER	PAYEE	TRANSACTION AMOUNT	OPEN BALANCE	PAYMENT
☑	03/06/2025	Invoice	1018	Sushi by	$80.00	$80.00	
☑	03/13/2025	Invoice	1023	Red	$70.00	$70.00	
☑	03/13/2025	Payment		55 Twin Lane	$50.00		

< First Previous 1-3 of 3 Next Last >

3 Selected transaction(s) Show | Remove	$200.00
Downloaded transaction	$200.00
Resolve 🔘 | Difference	$0.00
Total	$200.00

[Cancel] [Match]

» If QuickBooks doesn't suggest an automatic match, manually click the transaction, select Match, locate the invoice, and click Match.

Best Practice: Regularly reconciling these transactions prevents duplicates, discrepancies, and potential audit issues.

By diligently matching payments to invoices, you ensure accuracy, simplify future reconciliations, and enhance overall financial management efficiency.

IV. Understanding Undeposited Funds and Bank Deposits

1. What is Undeposited Funds (or Payments to Deposit)?

Think of Undeposited Funds or Payments to deposit as a virtual cash drawer.

When you receive multiple payments throughout the day—whether it's cash, checks, or card payments—you may deposit them together at the bank. Undeposited Funds holds those individual payments temporarily until you create a single bank deposit that matches your real-life bank activity.

Why it's useful:

- Helps match QuickBooks deposits to what's on your actual bank statement.
- Keeps multiple customer payments grouped together when deposited as one.
- Prevents your income from being overstated by double-posting transactions.

Best Practice: Always review your Undeposited Funds before making a bank deposit. If you skip this, QuickBooks may not match your bank feed later, making reconciliations messier than they need to be.

2. Which Transactions Can Use Undeposited Funds?

Not every payment in QuickBooks needs to go through the Undeposited Funds account—but many should.

Here are the most common types of transactions that post to it:

- Customer Payments (from invoices).
- Sales Receipts.
- Refund Receipts (in some cases).
- Credit Card or Check payments that are not immediately deposited.

Note: You don't need to use Undeposited Funds for transactions that are automatically downloaded from your banks if you've connected your banks and credit cards to QuickBooks.

3. Recording a Bank Deposit from Undeposited Funds

Once you're ready to take that batch of payments to the bank—or they've hit your merchant account—it's time to record the deposit properly. Here's how:

1. Click + Create > Select Bank Deposit.
2. Choose the Account:
   » Select the bank account the funds are being deposited into (e.g., Checking).
3. Select Payments:
   » You'll see a list of payments sitting in Undeposited Funds.

» Check the boxes next to the payments included in your actual bank deposit.

4. Add Bank Fees (if applicable):

» Scroll down to the Add funds to this deposit section.

» Enter negative amounts for merchant fees (e.g., Square or Stripe) using an expense category like "Bank Fees."

5. Review and Save:

» Double-check that the Total matches your actual bank statement.

» Click Save and Close.

Bank Deposit

Account: Checking — Balance $1,201.00
Date: 04/15/2025
AMOUNT: **$2,042.52**

Tags: Start typing to add a tag

Select the payments included in this deposit

RECEIVED FROM	DATE	TYPE	PAYMENT METHOD	MEMO	REF NO.	AMOUNT
Cool Cars	03/19/2025	Payment				$1,675.52
Freeman Sporting Goods:0969 Ocean View Road	03/19/2025	Payment				$387.00

1-2 of 2

Total: 2062.52
Selected Payments Total: 2062.52

Select all | Clear all

Add funds to this deposit

#	RECEIVED FROM	ACCOUNT	DESCRIPTION	PAYMENT METHOD	REF NO.	AMOUNT
1		Bank Charges				-$20.00
2						

Add lines | Clear all lines

Other funds total: -$20.00

Cancel | Clear | Print | Make recurring | Save and new

4. Reviewing Your Undeposited Funds Account

Want to know what's still sitting in your virtual drawer? Here's how to review what's in Undeposited Funds:

1. Go to the Chart of Accounts (Accounting > Chart of Accounts).

2. Find Undeposited Funds, then click View Register or Run Report.

3. You'll see all payments and collections in that account.

Use this view to:

• Spot old payments that were never deposited (and need attention).

- Troubleshoot why income isn't showing in your bank account.
- Stay on top of your cash flow.

Asset Register | Undeposited funds ⌄

$200.00

Go to: 1 of 1 ‹ First Previous **1-5 of 5** Next Last ›

▽ ▾ All

	REF NO. TYPE	PAYEE ACCOUNT	MEMO	DECREASE	INCREASE	✓ 🗂	BALANCE
Add deposit ▾							
12/28/2025		Lewis & Clark College			$200.00		$200.00
	Payment	Accounts receivable					
12/28/2025		Lewis & Clark College			$350.00	R	$0.00
	Payment	Accounts receivable					
12/28/2025		Client Sam			$100.00	R	-$350.00
	Payment	Accounts receivable					
12/28/2025		Client Sam		$100.00		R	-$450.00
	Deposit	Cash					
12/28/2025		Lewis & Clark College		$350.00		R	-$350.00
	Deposit	Cash					

Tip: Periodically review Undeposited Funds for stale transactions—especially during month-end. Anything that's been sitting there too long probably needs to be investigated.

V. Issuing Refunds, Credits, and Managing Returns

1. Processing Refunds for Customers

When you need to issue a refund, QuickBooks helps you handle it efficiently:

1. Navigate to Refund Receipts:
   » Click the + Create button.
   » Select Refund receipt under the Customers section.

2. Fill Out Refund Details:
   » Select the customer receiving the refund.
   » Enter refund details including date, payment method, and amount.
   » Specify the bank account from which the refund will be issued.

3. Record Refund Details:
   » Enter products or services being refunded and their quantities.
   » QuickBooks automatically calculates totals and adjusts inventory.

4. Save the Refund:

» Review your entries carefully.

» Click Save and Close or Save and Send if you want to email your customer to notify the refund.

Refund Receipt # 1007

Feedback

AMOUNT
$50.00

Customer	Email	Cc/Bcc
Alder Creek Winery	malder@aldercreekwin	

Billing Address
Alder Creek Winery
3487 NE Alder Creek Ln,
Newberg, OR 97132

Refund Receipt Date
04/11/2025

Refund Receipt no.
1007

Tags
Start typing to add a tag

Manage tags

Payment method
Credit Card

Refund From
Choose an account

Enter credit card details
Process credit card

#	SERVICE DATE	PRODUCT/SERVICE	DESCRIPTION	QTY	RATE	AMOUNT
1	04/10/2025	Event Consultation (hourly rate)	Event consulation	1	50	$50.00

2. Creating Credit Memos

Issuing a credit memo is often a practical alternative to cash refunds, particularly for product returns or service adjustments. Here's how to do it:

Credit Memo # 1007

Feedback

AMOUNT TO CREDIT
$150.00

Customer	Email	Cc/Bcc
Alder Creek Winery	malder@aldercreekwin	

Send later

Billing Address
Alder Creek Winery
3487 NE Alder Creek Ln,
Newberg, OR 97132

Credit Memo Date
04/11/2025

Credit Memo no.
1007

Tags
Start typing to add a tag

Manage tags

#	SERVICE DATE	PRODUCT/SERVICE	DESCRIPTION	QTY	RATE	AMOUNT
1	04/11/2025	Floral Supplies:Decorative Vase		10	15	$150.00
2						

Add lines   Clear all lines

Subtotal $150.00

Discount Percent   0.00 $0.00

Message displayed on credit memo

Cancel   Clear   Print or Preview | Make recurring   Save   Save and send

1. Navigate to Credit Memo Creation:
   - » Click + Create, then select Credit Memo under the Customers section.

2. Enter the Credit Memo Details:
   - » Select the customer to whom you're issuing the credit.
   - » Specify the date and list the products or services being credited. For product returns, enter each returned item's details carefully.

3. Review and Finalize:
   - » Double-check amounts and item descriptions before finalizing.
   - » Click Save and Close or Save and Send when details are verified.

Recommendation: Immediately send a copy of the credit memo to your customer. It confirms the credit available for future purchases, reducing potential confusion.

3. Managing Inventory with Returns

For businesses tracking inventory in QuickBooks, the good news is that inventory quantities adjust automatically when you issue a credit memo for returned products. Always review these automatic inventory adjustments:

- After creating the credit memo, verify your updated inventory numbers to ensure accuracy.
- Regular inventory checks are vital to maintain precise records and avoid discrepancies.

NAME ⬍	QTY ON HAND ⬍	AVAIL QTY ⬍	CATEGORY ⬍	SKU ⬍	TYPE ⬍	ACTION
Decorative Vase	60	60	Floral Supplies	FS VAS...	Inventory	Edit ❘ ⌄

Inventory quantity is automatically updated

Conduct regular inventory audits to confirm that physical stock matches QuickBooks records, especially after returns or adjustments.

Effectively managing credit memos and returns ensures clear financial records, accurate inventory counts, and maintains customer trust by handling these transactions promptly and professionally.

VI. Using Delayed Charge and Delayed Credit

In the real world, not every sale or discount happens immediately—and that's exactly why QuickBooks Online includes Delayed Charges and Delayed Credits. These tools let you record future revenue or future customer credits without affecting your books today.

If your business sends estimates, invoices at project completion, or offers credits that won't be applied until later, this section is for you.

1. What Are Delayed Charges and Delayed Credits?

Think of Delayed Charges as a reminder to invoice a customer later. You're tracking a service or product that was delivered (or will be), but you're not invoicing them just yet. For example: you provide event planning services for a client this month, but per agreement, you'll invoice everything at the end of the quarter. A delayed charge lets you log that revenue now—without affecting your income or receivables until you're ready.

Delayed Credits, on the other hand, represent a future discount or return you'll apply to a customer's account. For example: a client overpaid on a previous job, and you've agreed to apply that credit toward their next invoice. You can create a delayed credit to make sure it's not forgotten.

Note: If you're billing today or the discount applies immediately, do not use delayed charge or delayed credit, just use a standard Invoice or Credit Memo instead.

2. Creating a Delayed Charge

To create a delayed charge:

1. Go to + Create > Click Delayed Charge under Customers.
2. Enter the Customer Name.
3. Choose the Date: This is when the charge occurred, not necessarily when it will be invoiced.
4. Add the Product or Service:
   » Include quantity, rate, and description.

» Make sure the item is marked as taxable if it applies.

5. Save the delayed charge.

You've now created a reminder to bill your customer later—with all the necessary details stored safely.

3. Converting a Delayed Charge to an Invoice

When it's time to bill the customer, turning the delayed charge into an invoice is quick:

1. Go to + Create > Invoice.
2. Choose the Customer.
3. QuickBooks will prompt you to add the delayed charge to the invoice.
4. Review, make any adjustments, and click Review and Send (or Save and Close).

Pro Tip: You can also go to the Customer's profile, find the delayed charge, and convert it to an invoice directly from there.

4. Creating a Delayed Credit

Let's say you owe a customer a discount on a future invoice. Here's how to create a delayed credit:

1. Go to + Create > Click Delayed Credit under Customers.
2. Select the Customer and set the date.
3. Add the Product or Service, with a rate or amount to reflect the credit.
4. Include a Memo to explain the reason for the credit.
5. Save the transaction.

Again, this doesn't apply to any current invoice—it just waits in the background for when you're ready.

Customer   AMOUNT

Benson Hotel ⌄   **$200.00**

Delayed Credit Date   Delayed Credit no.

04/15/2025 📅   2

Tags ⑦   Manage tags

Start typing to add a tag

#	SERVICE DATE	PRODUCT/SERVICE	DESCRIPTION	QTY	RATE	AMOUNT	TAX	
⠿ 1	04/30/2025	Event Planning - Mini Package	Event Planning - Mini Package	1	200	$200.00	☐	🗑
⠿ 2							☐	🗑

Add lines   Clear all lines

       Total   **$200.00**

5. Applying a Delayed Credit to an Invoice

Now that your customer has a delayed credit, here's how to apply it:

1. Create an Invoice for the customer.
2. QuickBooks will ask if you want to apply the available delayed credit.
3. Click Add to apply it, and the total will automatically adjust.
4. Review and click Review and Send.

INVOICE   Balance due (hidden): **$0.00**

EverBloom Services   \@gmail.com

Knoxville.

Edit company

EverBloom
SERVICES

< **Suggested transactions**

We've found one or more transactions linked to Benson Hotel. Select the ones you'd like to add to the invoice.

▽ Filter   Add all

Benson Hotel ⌄ ✳

alex.martinez@bensonhotel.com

Cc/Bcc

Charge #1
Date: Apr 15, 2025
Total: $200.00
Notes: Event Planning - Mini Package   Add

Bill to	Location of Sale (hidden)		
Benson Hotel		Invoice no.	1010
309 SW Broadway, Portland, OR 97205		Terms	Net 30 ⌄
		Invoice date	04/15/2025 📅
		Due date	05/15/2025 📅

Edit Customer   Add shipping info

Credit #2
Date: Apr 15, 2025
Total: -$200.00
Notes: Event Planning - Mini Package   Add

This keeps the transaction history clear and your receivables up to date.

VII.   Entering and Managing Bills and Vendor Payments

Effectively managing your bills and vendor payments is crucial to maintaining accurate financial records and ensuring healthy cash flow. QuickBooks Online provides robust tools to help streamline this process efficiently.

1. Creating and Recording Bills

To accurately capture your expenses and obligations, follow these steps to enter new bills:

1. Navigate to Bill Entry:

   » Click + Create and select Bill under the Vendors section. Alternatively, access it via the Expenses > Bills menu, click Add Bill then click Create bill.

2. Enter Vendor and Bill Information:

   » Select your vendor from the dropdown menu. QuickBooks will auto-populate the vendor's mailing address if already saved.

   » Input relevant details such as the bill date, due date, payment terms, and the vendor's bill number to keep records organized and avoid duplicate payments.

   » QuickBooks also allows autofill the bills with files or images to reduce your manual input. You just need to review if the autofill information is correct.

3. Itemize Expenses Clearly:

   » Use the Category and Description fields to itemize each expense clearly. QuickBooks automatically totals your bill, simplifying calculations and accuracy checks.

4. Write Memo: Here you can document details about the bill.

5. Attach Supporting Documents (Recommended):

   » Utilize QuickBooks' convenient Autofill from file feature by uploading documents such as PDFs, PNGs, or JPEGs. QuickBooks will extract and autofill bill details, significantly reducing manual data entry and potential errors.

   » Alternatively, manually attach files under the Attachments section for future reference and audit trails.

6. Review and Save:

   » Carefully review all entered data.

   » Click Save or choose Save and schedule payment to take you to QuickBooks Bill Pay.

Entering bills immediately upon receipt ensures your financial reports remain accurate and your obligations clearly visible.

2. Scheduling and Tracking Bill Payments

Timely payment management is essential to maintain favorable vendor relationships and control your cash flow effectively. Here's how to manage payments smoothly in QuickBooks Online:

Bill #1001

Copy Give feedback ⚙ ? ✕

Supplier

Aaron Patel ⌄

BALANCE DUE

$200.00

Mailing address	Terms	Bill date	Due date	Bill no
Aaron Patel Dallas, TX	Net 30 ⌄	12/25/2025 📅	01/24/2026 📅	1001

#	CATEGORY	DESCRIPTION	AMOUNT
1	Legal and professional fees	Accounting Service	$200.00
2			
3			

Add lines   Clear all lines

Subtotal $200.00

Total $200.00

Memo

Cancel   Clear   Print   Make recurring   Save   Save and new ⌄

1. Access Bill Payment:

» Navigate to + Create and select Pay Bills.

» Alternatively, go directly to the Expenses > Bills menu. From here, you can filters the status of bills, bill date to narrow down which bills you want to view. Then click Pay Bills.

For review	**Unpaid**	Paid

Filters ⌄   Bill date: Last 12 months

Vendor   ✕

All ⌄

Bill date	From	To
Last 12 months ⌄	04/01/2024 📅	04/30/2025 📅

Reset   Apply

2. Select Bills to Pay:

» QuickBooks clearly displays a list of outstanding bills with critical details including vendor name, reference numbers, due dates, overdue status, and open balances.

» Select the bills by checking the boxes next to each entry.

3. Choose Payment Method and Account:

» Select the appropriate bank account from the Payment account dropdown.

» Confirm the payment date and starting check number, if applicable.

Pay Bills

						TOTAL PAYMENT AMOUNT
Payment account	Payment date	Starting check no.				
Checking	04/11/2025	71	Print later			**$291.44**
Balance: $1,201.00						

Filters ∨ · Last 12 months

	PAYEE	REF NO.	DUE DATE	STATUS	OPEN BALANCE	CREDIT APPLIED	PAYMENT	TOTAL AMOUNT
☑	PG&E		02/28/2025	Overdue 42 days ago	$86.44	Not available	86.44	$86.44
☑	Norton Lumber and Building Materials		03/15/2025	Overdue 27 days ago	$205.00	Not available	205.00	$205.00
☐	Robertson & Associates		03/15/2025	Overdue 27 days ago	$315.00	Not available	0.00	$0.00

Cancel · **Schedule payments** ∨

4. Schedule or Execute Payment:

» Click Schedule payment to schedule payments with your bank directly from QuickBooks, or choose Save and close or Save and print if you use different method.

Note: If you connect your banks and credit cards to QuickBooks, after the payment is cleared, QuickBooks will automatically match it for you. But I recommend you still review it manually periodically (weekly or monthly if you don't have many bills).

Regularly using QuickBooks for bill payments ensures accuracy, simplifies reconciliation, and helps you manage cash flow effectively.

3. Best Practices: Handling Late Payments and Early Discounts

QuickBooks provides intuitive features to manage scenarios like late payments or discounts offered by vendors:

- Address Late Payments Quickly:

» Regularly review overdue bills clearly marked in QuickBooks. Promptly addressing these helps maintain positive vendor relationships and good credit standings.

- Utilize Vendor Discounts:

» When vendors offer early payment discounts, enter these discounts either by adjusting the original bill amount or creating a vendor credit. Applying discounts correctly in QuickBooks maintains accurate records, reduces overall expenses, and enhances profitability.

Consistent and proactive management of bills, discounts, and payment scheduling ensures your business maintains robust financial health.

VIII.   Vendor Credits and Refunds

Every now and then, vendors issue refunds or credit memos for returned items, overpayments, or billing errors. Or maybe your credit card provider reverses a charge or gives a refund. Whatever the case, QuickBooks Online makes it easy to record these credits accurately—so your books stay clean and your payables reflect the real picture.

1. Vendor Credit – When a Supplier Owes You

Let's say your business returns items to a supplier or receives a discount or refund on a bill. Instead of handing you cash, most vendors issue a Vendor Credit—a balance you can apply to future bills.

When to Use a Vendor Credit:

- You returned products or canceled services.
- You were overcharged on a bill.
- The vendor issued a rebate or discount after you received the bill.
- You want to apply the credit to a future payment (not a refund to the bank).

2. How to Record a Vendor Credit:

1. Go to + Create > Choose Vendor Credit under the Vendors section.
2. Select the Vendor who issued the credit.

3. Enter the Credit Date (when you received the credit).
4. Enter the Details:
   » Add the product or service returned.
   » Input quantities and rates just like a bill—but as a credit.
   » Make sure to match categories (accounts) used on the original bill.
5. Save and Close.

QuickBooks now holds this credit to either offset a future bill or record a refund from that vendor.

3. Applying a Vendor Credit to a Bill

If you record bills from that vendor, you can use the credit recorded for future bill:

1. Go to + Create > Pay Bills.
2. Choose the vendor with an open bill.
3. When the bill opens, QuickBooks will automatically display available credits at the top.
4. Check the box to apply the vendor credit.
5. The total payment amount will adjust accordingly.
6. Choose your payment method and click Save and Close.

This reduces the amount owed to the vendor without manual math, and keeps your accounts payable accurate.

4. Applying a Vendor Credit to Bank Deposit

If the vendor issued a refund (cash, check, or bank transfer) and there won't be a future bill to offset it, you'll need to take a few extra steps to move the credit out of Accounts Payable.

Step 1: Record the Refund Transaction

1. Go to + Create > Bank Deposit.
2. In the Received From field, select the vendor name.
3. In the Account field, select Accounts Payable (A/P) – this is key!
4. Enter the payment method, date, and amount of the refund.
5. Click Save and Close.

This records the incoming funds and ties them to your A/P.

Step 2: Link the Deposit to the Vendor Credit

1. Go to + Create > Pay Bills.
2. Select the same vendor used in the steps above.
3. You'll see the Vendor Credit and the Bank Deposit listed.
4. Check both boxes to apply one against the other.
5. Make sure the amount applied equals zero, then click Save.

Pay Bills								⑦ ✕
								🗹 Give feedback
Payment account		Payment date		Starting check no.			TOTAL PAYMENT AMOUNT	
Checks ⌄		04/15/2025 📅		2		☐ Print later	**$0.00**	
Balance: $4,770.00								
Filters ⌄ Last 12 months								⚙
	PAYEE	REF NO.	DUE DATE	STATUS	OPEN BALANCE	CREDIT APPLIED	PAYMENT	TOTAL AMOUNT
☑	Internet		04/15/2025	Due today	$20.00	20.00	0.00	$20.00

This clears out the credit AND the deposit, without affecting your expenses or liabilities incorrectly.

IX. Managing Sales Tax in Transactions

Let's dive into what happens next—using that setup in your everyday transactions. Whether you're creating invoices, paying your collected taxes, or checking your tax reports, QuickBooks Online has your back every step of the way.

1. Applying and Adjusting Sales Tax on Invoices

Once you've enabled sales tax in QuickBooks Online, it works behind the scenes to calculate the correct rate based on where your sale is happening. That means less time calculating and more time focusing on your business.

But understanding how sales tax is applied—and how to adjust it when needed—is key to staying compliant and confident. Let's walk through how QuickBooks handles it, and what you should watch for.

1. How Sales Tax Is Applied to Invoice:

When creating an invoice in QBO, sales tax is calculated automatically based on a few key factors:

- **Customer's Location:** QuickBooks uses the shipping address on the invoice to determine the correct jurisdiction and rate. No shipping address? Then it falls back to the customer's primary address.

- **Taxable Items:** Only items that are marked as taxable in your Products and Services list will have sales tax applied. It's worth reviewing your list periodically to make sure every item is set up correctly.

Best Practice Tip: If you sell a mix of taxable and non-taxable items (like consulting + floral supplies), make sure each item is individually marked in its setup. It saves time and avoids mischarging tax.

2. Review Sales Tax:

When you create a new invoice and select a customer, QuickBooks does the heavy lifting:

- Customer location is used to determine which sales tax rates apply.
- The system checks if the customer is exempt or not.
- It calculates tax rates based on the sale address, pulling both state and local rates.
- Only taxable products and services contribute to the calculation.

You'll see this breakdown when you click "See the math" beside the Sales Tax line on your invoice.

How your sales tax is calculated: ✕

Customer — Edit
- This customer is not tax-exempt

Location and addresses — Edit

Location of Sale — **Knoxville,**

Based on this address you need to collect sales tax for these agencies:

Tennessee Department of Revenue

Tennessee State	7%
Tennessee, Knoxville City	2.25%
Total rate	9.25%

Products and services — Edit

Manage the tax rates being applied to each line item on your invoice:

PRODUCT	SALES TAX AMOUNT
˅ Boutonniere & Corsage (Set)	$23.13
Uncategorized - standard rate applied	

AGENCY	TAXABLE AMOUNT	TAX RATE	SALES TAX TOTAL
Tennessee State	250.00	7%	17.50
Tennessee, Knoxville City	250.00	2.25%	5.63

Total sales tax	$23.13

3. Adjusting Sales Tax Manually (When Needed):

While automation is ideal, there are times you may need to override or adjust the tax.

Add a custom sales tax rate ✕

- Click Override this amount at the bottom of the breakdown window if you've selected Automatic Calculation. Or:

  ◉ Single
  ○ Combined

  Name
  [   ]

- Select Add rate in the sales tax rate dropdown, then manually select custom rate for that invoice.

  Agency
  [Select one   ⌄]

4. Save and Send:

  Rate
  [0   %]

- Click Save and Send to email it directly to your customer or Save and Close if you want to send it later.

It's that easy—and you'll never have to manually calculate tax again!

2. Managing Sales Tax Payments

Collecting sales tax is just the beginning—you also need to track it and pay it on time. QuickBooks makes this stress-free:

1. Go to the Sales Tax Center:

- Click Taxes on the left-hand menu, then click on Sales Tax.
  » You'll see how much sales tax you've collected and when it's due.

2. Review What You Owe:

- QuickBooks tracks how much you've collected for each tax agency.
  » You'll see clear due dates and amounts—no guesswork involved.

3. Record a Payment:

- When you're ready to remit the tax, click Record Tax Payment.
  » Select the tax agency, payment account, and payment date.
  » Enter the amount paid and click Save and Close.

Timely tax payments help you avoid penalties—and QuickBooks makes sure you stay ahead of the game.

3. Review Sales Tax

Sales tax reports help you stay audit-ready and give you a clear view of your obligations. Let's explore how to use them:

1. Access Reports:

- Go to All apps > Sales Tax > Overview.

2. View reports:

- By default, QBO prepares some charts: Sales Tax Due, Sales Tax Accuring, Unpaid Tax Returns. Use those charts to review how much tax you've collected.

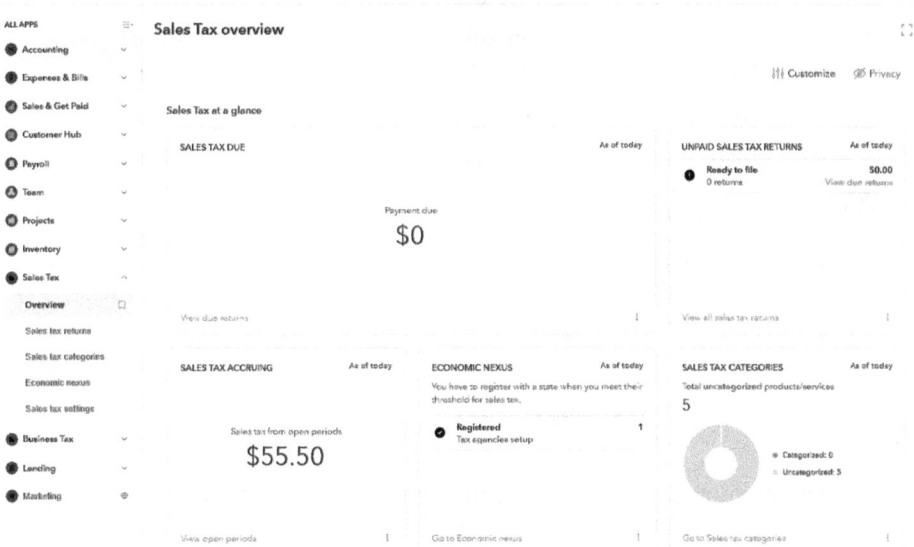

- Use the report to fill in state tax return, or provide it to your accountant.

With clear reporting and automated tracking, you'll be ready to handle tax season with calm confidence.

X. Expense Receipts Management

Whether you're grabbing coffee for a client meeting, stocking up on supplies, or paying for a venue rental—every business purchase leaves a trail. And in QuickBooks Online, managing those receipts isn't just about staying organized. It's about tying every dollar to a clear, accurate record.

Here's how to handle your receipts the right way—without the paper clutter.

1. Uploading Receipts to QuickBooks

QuickBooks makes it easy to capture receipts no matter where you are or how you receive them. Choose the method that works best for your workflow:

1. Snap and Upload on Mobile

» Open the QuickBooks mobile app.

» Tap the Menu icon > choose Receipt Snap.

» Take a clear photo of your receipt and submit.

» QuickBooks automatically extracts the key details like amount, date, and vendor.

2. Upload from Your Computer or Google Drive

» Go to the All apps > Accounting > Receipts.

» Click Upload receipts, then select Upload receipts if you want to upload from your computer, or Upload from Google Drive.

» Drag and drop the files, or select the receipts from your Google Drive.

» QuickBooks will analyze the receipt and begin processing it.

3. Forward by Email

» QuickBooks automatically creates two unique emails for you to use to autofill multiple receipts or invoices. You can even edit these emails to make them best suit your needs.

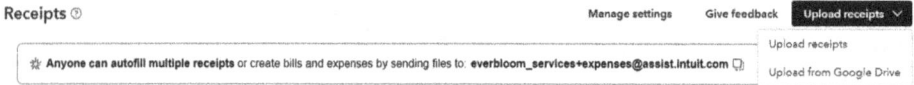

Receipts ⓘ

Manage settings   Give feedback   **Upload receipts** ⌄

Upload receipts

⚡ **Anyone can autofill multiple receipts** or create bills and expenses by sending files to: **everbloom_services+expenses@assist.intuit.com** 🗗

Upload from Google Drive

» From your email inbox, forward any e-receipt (PDF or image format) to your QuickBooks receipt address.

2. Reviewing, Matching and Categorizing Uploaded Receipts

Once your receipt is in QuickBooks, it's time to verify the data and make it work for your books. There are 2 scenarios for your receipt: it can be already in your books or it has not.

If the transaction has already existed in your books, QuickBooks will prompt you to match it. If it doesn't, you can manually search for the transactions to match. Once matched, the receipt moves to Reviewed and it is attached permanently.

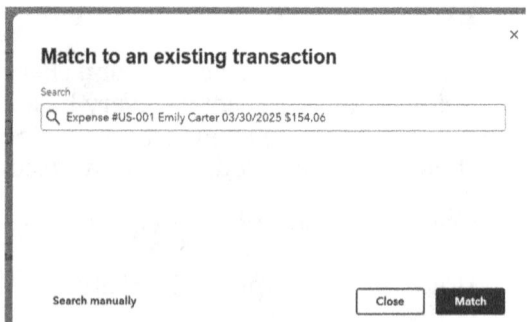

×

Match to an existing transaction

Search

🔍 Expense #US-001 Emily Carter 03/30/2025 $154.06

Search manually   Close   Match

If QuickBooks cannot find an existing transaction that matches, you can review and create the new transaction directly from your receipt.

QuickBooks will suggest:

- Transaction Type.
- Payee.
- Payment Date and Amount Paid.
- Expense Category and Description.

Make sure you double-check the suggested information before confirming.

What to Look For:

- Correct vendor name? Matches your Chart of Accounts?
- Expense category accurate? Choose wisely—this impacts reporting, deductions, and budgeting.

You can also add a memo and attachments to the transaction—great for clarifying purchases or justifying business purpose later.

XI. Writing and Printing Checks

Let's now focus on the process of writing and printing checks in QuickBooks Online. Checks differ from bills or electronic payments, which typically handle recurring or credit-based transactions. Even in a digital world, checks remain vital, and QuickBooks makes issuing checks simple, organized, and secure.

1. Step-by-Step Check Creation

Follow these straightforward steps to write checks in QuickBooks Online:

1. Initiate Check Creation:

» Click + Create. Under the Vendors section, select Check.

2. Enter Check Details:

» Choose an existing vendor (payee) or create a new one directly in the form.

» Specify the bank account you're writing the check from.

» Fill in the check date and payment amount clearly.

3. Itemize Expenses or Purchases:

» Enter the category, description, and amounts of expenses or products/services associated with the check. Precise categorization ensures accurate financial reporting.

4. Review and Save:

» Confirm all details carefully for accuracy.

» Select Save and Close to finalize or Print check if you wish to immediately print the check.

You've now effectively recorded your check, providing a clear audit trail and maintaining accurate financial records. Next, we will take a look on how to properly print your checks.

2. Printing Checks – Best Practices and Setup

Properly printed checks enhance professionalism and reduce errors. QuickBooks Online guides you through an intuitive setup to ensure each check prints correctly:

1. Navigate to Check Printing Setup:

   » Click on the New button on the left side, then choose Print Checks under the Vendors section.

   » Click Print Setup to start configuring the setup process.

2. Select Check Type:

   » Choose the check layout that matches your pre-printed checks—typically either Voucher (one check per page with vouchers) or Standard (three checks per page).

   » Click View preview and print sample to generate a test print on blank paper.

   » If the test print is not properly setup, move to step 3.

3. Set Up PDF Reader:

   » Ensure Adobe Reader is installed and set as the default PDF viewer, providing consistent and accurate alignment when printing.

   » Generate a test print. If the test print still isn't properly setup, move to step 4.

4. Align and Adjust Checks:

   » Follow the prompts to fine-tune the alignment by dragging the grid so your printed checks align correctly with the pre-printed paper stock.

   » Run additional print tests if necessary, making slight horizontal or vertical adjustments until perfect alignment is achieved.

5. Finalize Setup:

   » Once aligned correctly, click Finish setup. Your QuickBooks Online account will save these settings for consistent results in future prints.

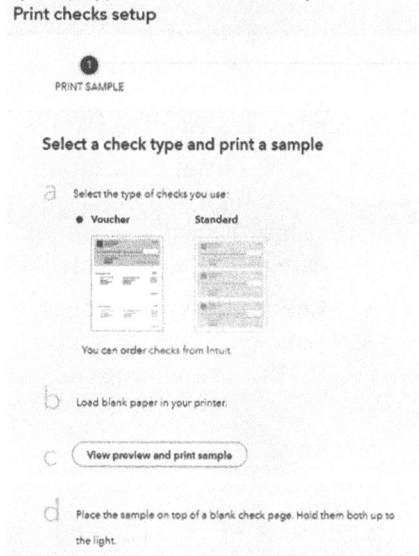

XII.   Handling Recurring Transactions and Expenses in QuickBooks Online

Managing recurring transactions effectively is key to maintaining predictable cash flow, reducing administrative burdens, and keeping your books accurate. I recommend utilizing QuickBooks Online's recurring transaction features to automate regular financial activities.

1. Setting Up Recurring Transactions

Follow these steps to seamlessly automate routine transactions in QuickBooks:

1. Access Recurring Transactions:
   » Go to Accounting > Recurring Transactions.

2. Create a New Recurring Transaction:
   » Click New and select the type of transaction you wish to automate (Invoice, Bill, Expense, etc.).

3. Specify Transaction Details:
   » Clearly enter the required information, including the vendor or customer name, transaction amount, account/category, and a detailed description.
   » Choose the recurrence frequency (weekly, monthly, annually) and set appropriate start and end dates for the automation.

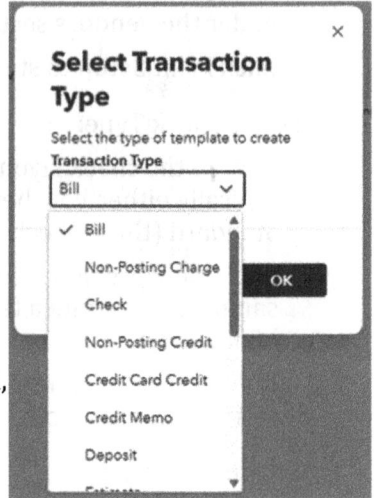

Select Transaction Type

Select the type of template to create

Transaction Type

Bill

✓ Bill

Non-Posting Charge

Check

Non-Posting Credit

Credit Card Credit

Credit Memo

Deposit

OK

Recurring Check

Template name | Type
Scheduled | Create | days in advance

Payee
Who did you pay? | Bank Account | Checks

Interval
Monthly | on | day | 1st | of every | 1 | month(s) | Start date MM/DD/YYYY | End None

Mailing address | Check no. | To print | ✓ Print later

Tags | Manage tags
Start typing to add a tag

#	CATEGORY	DESCRIPTION	AMOUNT
1			
2			

Add lines | Clear all lines | Total | $0.00

Cancel | Save template

» You can also autofill some templates like bills, invoices with files and images from your device.

4. Review and Activate:

» Carefully review all details to ensure accuracy.

» Click Save Template to activate and schedule your recurring transaction.

Automating these transactions not only saves valuable administrative time but also significantly reduces the risk of manual errors.

2. Editing and Deleting Recurring Transactions

Business conditions often change, and QuickBooks allows flexibility to easily update or discontinue recurring transactions:

To Edit a Recurring Transaction:

1. Navigate to Accounting > Recurring Transactions.
2. Identify the transaction requiring adjustments, then click Edit.
3. Update essential details—amount, dates, frequency, or account information—as needed.
4. After review, click Save Template to confirm your updates.

Recurring Transactions
‹ All Lists   Give feedback   Reminder List ∨   New

| Filter by Name | Filter | All | | | | | Manage recurring payments | |

TEMPLATE NAME ▲	TYPE	TXN TYPE	INTERVAL	PREVIOUS DATE	NEXT DATE	CUSTOMER/VENDOR	AMOUNT	ACTION
Monthly Building Lease	Scheduled	Bill	Every Month		03/30/2025	Hall Properties	900.00	Edit ▾
Telephone Bill	Scheduled	Bill	Every Month		03/30/2025	Cal Telephone	74.36	Edit ▾

To Delete a Recurring Transaction:

1. Open Recurring Transactions.
2. Locate the transaction you want to remove, click the dropdown arrow next to Edit, and select Delete.
3. Confirm your action to remove the scheduled transaction permanently.

Consistently maintaining your recurring transactions ensures your financial data remains accurate and aligned with your current operational realities.

3. Best Practices for Managing Recurring Expenses

To optimize your use of recurring transactions and enhance your business's financial efficiency, adopt these recommended practices:

- Regular Transaction Reviews: Periodically audit your recurring transactions to verify their accuracy, relevance, and necessity, ensuring outdated or unnecessary payments don't go unnoticed.
- Provide Clear and Detailed Descriptions: Including precise descriptions and notes simplifies future transaction reviews and audits, making expense management more transparent.
- Define Clear Start and End Dates: Always set definitive start and end dates, particularly for limited-term or seasonal expenses, to avoid unintended payments.
- Monitor Cash Flow Regularly: Track recurring payments closely, ensuring they align comfortably within your budget, cash flow projections, and financial objectives.

Adhering to these best practices supports proactive financial management, enhances your budgeting accuracy, and reduces administrative stress— allowing you to focus on strategic growth and profitability.

CHAPTER 5: PAYROLL AND EMPLOYEE MANAGEMENT

I. Setting Up Payroll in QuickBooks Online

If you're ready to take payroll off your to-do list and do it right from the start—this section is for you! QuickBooks Online makes it easy to pay your team, stay compliant, and feel confident knowing your payroll is accurate and stress-free. Let's walk through the steps to set everything up smoothly.

1. Choosing the Right Payroll Service

QuickBooks Online offers multiple payroll plans. Picking the one that fits your business needs will set you up for success:

- Core: Ideal for small teams. Includes full-service payroll, tax filing, and direct deposit.
- Premium: Adds features like same-day direct deposit, time tracking, and HR support.
- Elite: Best for larger or growing teams. Includes expert setup, tax penalty protection, and more advanced HR tools.

Tip: You can always upgrade later as your business grows.

2. Gathering Required Employee Information

Before running payroll, you'll need to collect some key details for each employee. Having these ready will make setup go much faster:

- Full legal name and home address
- Social Security number (SSN)
- Date of birth and hire date
- W-4 form (tax withholding preferences)
- Pay rate and schedule (hourly/salary, weekly/biweekly, etc.)
- Bank account info (for direct deposit)

You can enter this manually or send employees a link to fill it out securely through QuickBooks.

3. Completing Initial Payroll Setup

Now it's time to set the wheels in motion!

  1. Go to Payroll Settings:

- Click All apps > Payroll > Overview in the left-hand menu.
  » Select Get Started or Set Up Payroll if you haven't already.

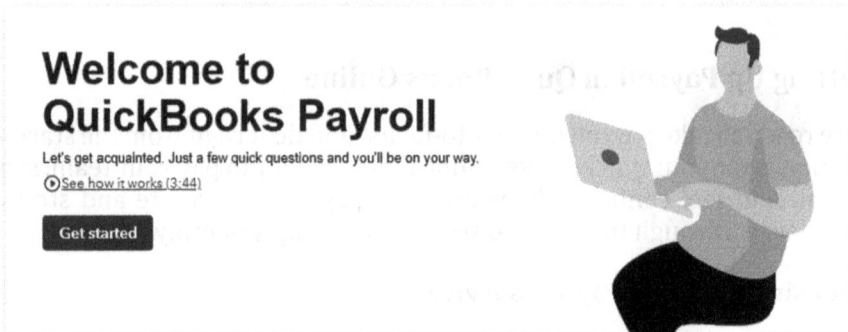

Welcome to QuickBooks Payroll

Let's get acquainted. Just a few quick questions and you'll be on your way.

▶ See how it works (3:44)

Get started

2. Get Ready to Pay Your Team

- Confirm Payday: Ensure your payday schedule aligns with your cash flow. QuickBooks will mark your calendar with the first payday.
- Enter Your Business Information: Verify your primary business location and set up your payroll contact. Accuracy here supports compliance and seamless communication.

SETUP TASKS

1 **Get ready to pay your team**   2 tasks left ∧

✓ **Payday is set**
We have your first payday on the calendar.

✓ **Your business info is complete**
Your primary work location and payroll contact are set.

○ **Tell us about your team**
Enter each employee's info to get them ready for payday.   Start

○ **Connect your bank**
Use next-day direct deposit and pay your taxes electronically.   Start

SETUP RESOURCES

Check out all our help videos and list of documents to have on hand.

▣ View setup guide

Get ready to pay your team ∧

▶ Set up your team (4:32)
▶ Connect your bank account (1:51)
▶ Run payroll with direct deposit (2:34)

Let us handle your taxes ∨

- Enter Employee Information:
  » Click Start under "Tell us about your team." Provide essential employee details such as addresses, salary, pay rates, and withholding information.
  » You can provide these information by importing from Run by ADP, Gusto, Paychex, from a spreadsheet or manually inputting.
  » You can also review and edit all the information of an employee by

clicking the employee's name. QuickBooks allows you to store detailed information about employees: pay type (hourly, overtime, bonus, comission, etc.), record time off, record deductions and contributions and emergency contact.

Edit employee

Base pay			✏ Edit
Pay type	Rate	Default working hours	
Hourly	$18.00/hour	40.00 hours/week	

Additional pay types			⊕ Add
Pay type			
Type... ⌄			

PAY TYPE	NAME	RATE/AMOUNT	ACTIONS
Overtime Pay	Overtime Pay	1.5x base pay	Edit ｜ ⌄

Time off — Start
Set up time off policies like sick pay and vacation for eligible employees.

Deductions and contributions — Start
Include paycheck deductions and company contributions for healthcare and retirement. Garnishments too.

Emergency contact — Start
Employee's contact in case of emergency. This could be their spouse, partner, or friend.

- Connect Your Bank: Link your business bank account to facilitate direct deposits and automated tax payments, streamlining your payroll disbursements.

3. Setting Up Your Payroll Taxes:

- Enter Your Tax Information: Have your state and federal tax IDs ready. Enter this information accurately to ensure timely tax filings and avoid late penalties.

- Establish Tax Preferences: Set your preferences clearly—choose whether QuickBooks should manage tax filings automatically or if you'll handle them yourself. Using automated tax management is generally recommended to save time and reduce errors.

- Connect Your Bank for Taxes: If you haven't already, link your bank account for electronic payroll tax payments. This connection facilitates timely tax remittances and minimizes the risk of missed payments..

4. Taking Care of Your Team:

- Workers' Compensation Policy: Set up your workers' compensation policy promptly. Compliance here is vital for protecting both your business and your team in the event of workplace incidents.

- Explore 401(k) Plans: Offering retirement benefits such as 401(k) plans attracts and retains talent, positioning your business as a competitive and employee-friendly workplace.

- Employee Health Plans: QuickBooks integrates employee health plans with payroll, making benefit administration simpler. Regularly review affordable options to maintain employee satisfaction and compliance with healthcare requirements.

(3) Take care of your team 3 tasks left ∧

Add a workers' comp policy

Comply with state law and protect your business. Due as soon as you hire your first employee.

Start

Explore 401(k) plans

401(k) plans are a great way to attract and retain talent while helping your team save for the future.

Start

Check out employee health plans

Take care of your team with a plan that integrates with your payroll. Compare affordable quotes from top providers.

Start

Recommendations

- Regularly verify employee information, especially tax details, to maintain accurate payroll records and ensure compliance.

- Set clear calendar reminders or leverage QuickBooks' automated alerts to never miss a payday or tax filing deadline.

- Review and reconcile payroll expenses frequently. This practice ensures financial clarity and helps you manage business cash flow efficiently.

By thoughtfully completing these payroll setup tasks, you'll streamline your payroll management, stay compliant with payroll regulations, and confidently manage employee compensation and benefits.

II. Managing Employee Payments and Direct Deposits

With your payroll all set up, it's time for the exciting part—paying your employees! QuickBooks Online makes this process smooth, accurate, and fast. Whether you're paying weekly or biweekly, by check or direct deposit, this section will show you how to confidently manage every payroll run with ease.

1. Scheduling Payroll Runs

Your pay schedule sets the rhythm of your payroll process. Here's how to manage it like a pro:

1. Go to the Payroll Dashboard:

- Click All Apps > Payroll > Employees then click Run payroll.

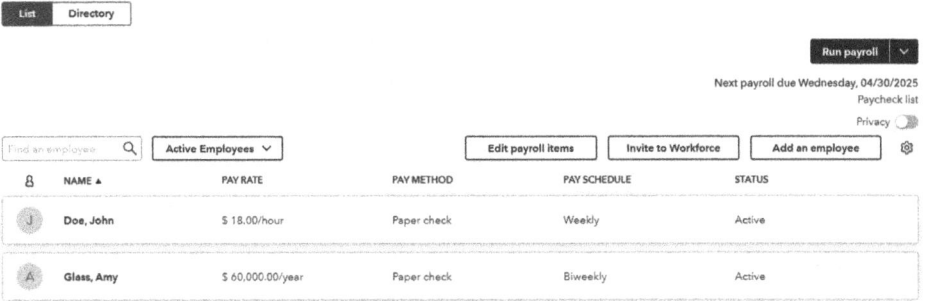

2. Select a pay schedule.

- Depending on your employee information that you've imported or inputted, you can select a pay schedule for such payroll run.

Select a pay schedule for this payroll

◉ Biweekly (1 employee)
   Next pay date: 04/30/2025

◯ Weekly (1 employee)
   Next pay date: 04/30/2025

3. Review Pay Dates and Periods:

- Make sure the pay period and pay date are correct. Adjust if needed.

4. Review and Edit Employee Hours and Pay:

- For hourly employees, enter the number of hours worked.
- For salaried employees, QuickBooks will calculate the pay automatically. You can also edit hours worked and paycheck manually.

5. Edit Paycheck if Needed:

If you ever need to edit the paycheck, depending on your employee types, you can edit some information (such as overtime hours, employee federal income tax) directly in the paycheck before you send it out.

PAY TO

NET PAY

Amy Glass

$1,932.63

Employee address	Pay date	Pay period
123 1/2 14th Ave N	04/16/2025	04/05/2025 to 04/18/2025
Saint Petersburg, FL 33701-	**Paid from**	**Paid by**
1105		Check ($1,932.63)

˅ Pay

TYPE	Hours	Rate	Current	YTD
Salary			$2,307.69	$2,307.69
Overtime Pay	0.00	$ 43.27	$0.00	$0.00
Total			**$2,307.69**	**$2,307.69**

˅ Employee taxes

TYPE	Current	YTD
Federal Income Tax	$ 198.52	$198.52
Social Security	$143.08	$143.08
Medicare	$33.46	$33.46
Total	**$375.06**	**$375.06**

Close

Save

6. Preview and Confirm:

TOTAL PAYROLL COST

$2,498.08	Funding account --	Pay period: 04/05/2025 to 04/18/2025	
		Pay date: 04/16/2025	
Gross pay	$2,307.69	Chart of account	
Employer taxes & contributions	$190.39	Checks ˅	

Name (1) ▲	Total hours	Gross pay	Employee taxes & deductions	Net pay	Employer taxes & contributions	Change in gross pay	Memo
Glass, Amy $60,000.00/year Paper check	80h	$2,307.69	$375.06	$1,932.63 🔍	$190.39	– ⓘ	+ New memo
Total	80h	$2,307.69	$375.06	$1,932.63	$190.39		

- Click Preview payroll details to view all details relating to it. QuickBooks will prompt a new window to display all the payroll details. You can print it or save it as PDF.

- Once you are happy with the preview, click Submit payroll. Depending on the payment method you've set up, you can either pay your employee through direct deposit or write a paper check.

	Pay	Hours	Amount	Deductions	Amount	Employee taxes	Amount	Employer taxes	Amount
Amy Glass Net pay $1,932.63 Pay date: 04/16/2025 04/05/2025 - 04/18/2025	Salary	80	$2,307.69			Federal Income Tax	$198.52	FUTA Employer	$13.85
	Overtime Pay	0	$0.00			Social Security	$143.08	Social Security Employer	$143.08
						Medicare	$33.46	Medicare Employer	$33.46
								TN SUI Employer	$0.00
			$2,307.69						
				Total					
Net pay **$1,932.63**	Salary	80	$2,307.69			Federal Income Tax	$198.52	FUTA Employer	$13.85
	Overtime Pay	0	$0.00			Social Security	$143.08	Social Security Employer	$143.08
						Medicare	$33.46	Medicare Employer	$33.46
								TN SUI Employer	$0.00
				Total payroll cost					
Net pay **$1,932.63**		80	$2,307.69		$0.00		$375.06		$190.39

You've now completed a full payroll run—great job!

2. Setting Up Direct Deposit for Employees

Direct deposit saves time, improves accuracy, and keeps your team happy. Direct deposit only works if you have a US bank account that's set up for ACH transactions. Once you connect your bank account to QuickBooks and complete verification (if any), here's how to enable direct deposit for your employees:

1. Collect Employee Bank Info:

- You can enter the details yourself or invite employees to enter them securely.

2. Enable Direct Deposit:

- Go to Payroll, then Employees. Select the employee's name.
- Click Edit on the Payment method, then select Direct Deposit from the dropdown.
- Enter your employee's account and routing numbers.

3. Save the Info:

- Once you are done, click Save.

Direct deposit method

| Deposit to one account | ⌄ |

Bank account type

| Checking | ⌄ |

Routing number

| | |

Account number

| |

Confirm account number

| |

You're all set! On payday, funds go straight to your employees—no checks, no hassle.

III. Payroll Taxes and Compliance Essentials

When you run payroll, you're not just cutting checks—you're also stepping into the role of a tax collector for the government. Whether you're paying your first employee or your fiftieth, understanding your payroll tax responsibilities isn't optional—it's essential. QuickBooks Online does a lot of the heavy lifting, but you still need to know what you're responsible for.

Let's break it all down.

1. What Are Payroll Taxes?

Payroll taxes are the mandatory taxes that both you and your employees pay based on employee wages. They fall into two main categories:

a. Employee Withholdings (taken out of the employee's paycheck)

- Federal Income Tax: Based on the employee's W-4 form and federal tax brackets.
- State and Local Income Tax: If your state or city requires it.
- FICA (Federal Insurance Contributions Act):
  » Social Security: 6.2% withheld from employee wages.
  » Medicare: 1.45% withheld (additional 0.9% for employees earning over $200,000).

b. Employer Contributions (paid by you, the employer):

- FICA Match: You match the employee's Social Security and Medicare contributions (another 6.2% + 1.45%)
- FUTA (Federal Unemployment Tax Act):
  » 6.0% on the first $7,000 of each employee's annual wages
  » In most cases, you get a credit of up to 5.4%, making the effective FUTA rate 0.6%.
- SUTA (State Unemployment Tax):
  » Rates and wage limits vary by state—QuickBooks will prompt you to set this up based on your business location.

2. How Do You Know What You're Responsible For?

It depends on your business location and structure, but here are general rules:

1. Do you have employees?
   » You must withhold and remit federal income tax, Social Security, Medicare, and FUTA (plus state-level equivalents).
2. Are you in a state with income tax or unemployment tax?
   » You'll likely be responsible for SUTA and possibly withholding state income tax.
3. Are you hiring contractors?
   » Different rules apply—you usually don't withhold payroll taxes but may need to file 1099s instead (covered later in this chapter).

QuickBooks Payroll helps determine your obligations automatically during setup, but it's a good idea to double-check with your state's department of revenue and employment agency.

3. When Do You Pay and File?

According to the IRS Employer's Tax Guide, businesses must follow one of two deposit schedules for Social Security, Medicare, and federal income taxes: monthly or semi-weekly.

Here's a breakdown of the deposit due dates for employer payroll taxes, depending on the required deposit schedule:

- Monthly deposits: These are due by the 15th day of the following month. Applies if: You reported $50,000 or less in payroll tax liability during the lookback period (generally the four quarters ending the previous June 30).

- Semi-weekly deposits: For payments made Wednesday through Friday, deposits are due by the following Wednesday. For payments made Saturday through Tuesday, deposits are due by the following Friday. Applies if: You reported more than $50,000 in payroll tax liability during the lookback period. (Note: Your deposit schedule is based on your total tax liability, not your payroll frequency).

- Next-Day Deposit Rule (Special Case): If you accumulate $100,000 or more in tax liability on any day, you must deposit the tax by the next business day, regardless of your normal schedule.

- Some employers with very minimal payroll tax liabilities (under $2,500 for the quarter) might be on a quarterly schedule and taxes should be deposited by January 31, April 30, July 31, and October 31. The deposit schedule you'll use depends on your tax liability (not how often your employees are paid).

- FUTA tax has its own quarterly deposit rules: Due if your FUTA liability exceeds $500 in a quarter. Deposit due: By the last day of the month following the quarter: April 30, July 31, October 31, January 31. If your total FUTA liability is $500 or less in a quarter, carry it forward to the next quarter until it exceeds $500 or until the end of the year.

- State Payroll Taxes: Each state sets its own deposit rules and schedules. You'll need to check with your state's Department of Revenue or Department of Labor for accurate due dates.

Tip: QuickBooks Online Payroll (Core, Premium, or Elite) calculates, withholds, files, and even pays these taxes for you, so you stay compliant automatically. But it's still good to understand what's happening behind the scenes.

4. Setting Up Tax Withholding and Automatic Payments

QuickBooks Online helps you stay ahead of tax deadlines by automating withholdings and payments. Here's how to set it up right:

1. Go to Payroll Tax Setup:

- Click Payroll, then choose Payroll Tax from the left-hand menu.

2. Add Federal Tax Agency Info:

- Enter your federal EIN.
- Select the payroll tax form you file with IRS (most common is form 941).
- Confirm your tax deposit schedule (monthly, semi-weekly, etc.) based on your agency's instructions.

3. Add State Tax Info:

- Enter any required state tax account numbers for your business and where your employees live and work, SUI, UI rates.

- Confirm your tax deposit schedule (monthly, semi-weekly, etc.).

Give us your federal tax info

Once we have your tax info, we can correctly pay and file your federal taxes. You can find what you need in letters and tax notices you've received from the IRS.

Employer Identification Number (EIN) ⓘ

```
12-3456789
```

Apply for an EIN

Which payroll tax form do you file with the IRS? ⓘ

```
Form 941 each quarter (most common)      ⌄
```

What form do I use and can I switch later?

How often do you pay your taxes?

```
Semi-weekly (Recommended)      ⌄
```

We recommend semi-weekly or monthly payments to avoid tax penalty

4. Enable Auto Tax Payments and Filings:

- QuickBooks lets you opt-in to automatic payments and filings.
- This feature is on by default, but check it anyway. Find it in the Tax Settings section.

Let's add your Tennessee tax info

We'll need the following info to correctly pay and file your state payroll taxes based on where your employees live and work. You can find what you need in emails or letters you've received from the state. Learn more

Unemployment Insurance (UI)

Employer Account Number ⓘ

```
0123-565 8
```

Get your account number

SUI Additional Fee rate

```
0%      ⌄
```

Do you know your Unemployment Insurance (UI) rate? ⓘ

🔘 Yes, it's `2.7%` .

⚪ No, use 10% for now.

Jobs Skills Fee rate

```
0%      ⌄
```

5. Verify Employee Withholdings:

- Go to Employees, select a team member, and review their W-4 details.
- Make sure withholding allowances and filing status are accurate.

With just a few steps, you're on your way to hands-free payroll tax compliance!

5. Filing and Paying Payroll Tax in QBO

QuickBooks can prepare and file most federal and state payroll tax forms for you. Here's how to stay on top of the process:

1. Track Tax Forms and Due Dates:

- From the Payroll Tax Center, you'll see upcoming form deadlines like 941 (quarterly) and 940 (annual FUTA).
- Switch between Payments and Filings tabs to view the forms.
- QuickBooks automatically schedules them and reminds you before they're due.

2. Review and Approve Forms and Make Payment:

- If auto-filing is enabled, QuickBooks will notify you when forms are ready to file. Review the forms for accuracy and click Approve to file, or set them to auto-submit.
- Click Pay to pay payroll taxes. Depending on the payment method you've set up, you will be directed accordingly.

3. Maintain Filing Records:

- Once filed, QuickBooks saves copies of all forms and payment confirmations.
- You can download or print them anytime for your records or CPA.

IV. Managing and Paying 1099 Contractors

Independent contractors are an essential part of many small businesses—whether you're hiring a freelance photographer for an event or a landscaping crew to set up a venue. QuickBooks Online (QBO) makes it easier than ever to track what you pay them and ensure you're meeting IRS requirements when tax time comes around. Here's everything you need to know about setting up and managing 1099 contractors in QBO.

1. Who Needs a 1099? Understanding Contractors vs. Vendors

Let's clear up the basics first—because not every vendor is a 1099 contractor.

- 1099 contractors are non-employees you pay $600 or more during the year for services (not goods). This could include freelancers, consultants, designers, or subcontractors.
- Vendors in general may sell you products or services—but only contractors who meet the IRS criteria need a 1099.

Best Practice: If you pay someone via a third-party app like PayPal or a credit card, you're generally off the hook for issuing a 1099—the payment processor handles it under Form 1099-K. But if you're paying by check, ACH, or direct deposit, you're responsible.

2. What QuickBooks Online Can Track for You

QBO doesn't just help you send 1099s at year-end—it tracks your payments to contractors throughout the year and flags who qualifies for a 1099 based on how and how much you've paid them.

With QuickBooks, you can:

- Designate vendors as 1099 contractors
- Track all payments made by check, bank transfer, or direct deposit
- Run real-time 1099 summaries
- Prepare and e-file 1099-NEC and 1099-MISC forms
- Invite contractors to fill out their own W-9 and view their payment history via QuickBooks Contractor Portal

That's peace of mind, year-round.

3. How to Add a Contractor in QBO

Adding a contractor is just like adding a vendor—with a few extra details:

1. Go to Payroll > Contractors, or use Expenses > Vendors, then click Add a contractor.

2. Enter contractor details:

   » Name and email address.

3. Invite them to fill out their W-9 (recommended):

   » Check the box to email the contractor a secure link where they can submit their tax info. This keeps your records clean and your files audit-ready.

   » Contractor receives email to create a free account to fill out W-9 form.

4. Alternatively, don't click the email box and you can enter the contractor info manually.

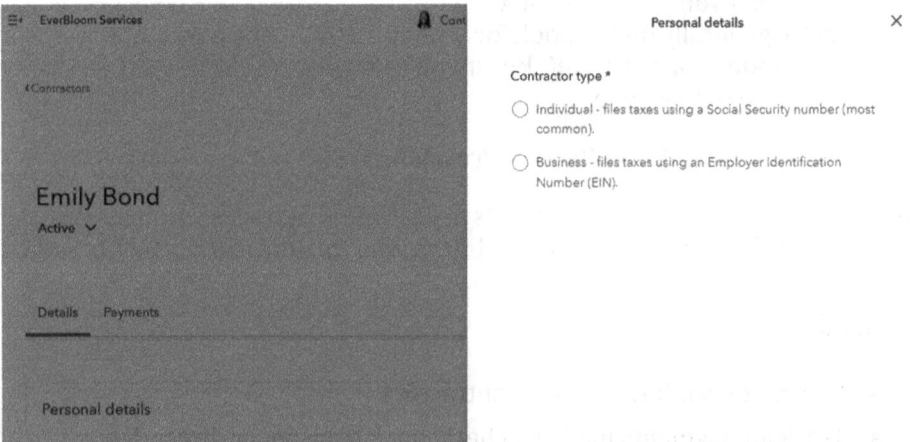

INTUIT quickbooks

EverBloom Services needs your W-9 info

Create a free account to share your details.
If you already have an account, just sign in.

Get started

Stay tax time ready

Keep a record of your tax forms and get your 1099s as soon as they're ready.

EverBloom Services | Cont

‹ Contractors

Emily Bond

Active ⌄

Details   Payments

Personal details

Personal details   ✕

Contractor type *

○ Individual - files taxes using a Social Security number (most common).

○ Business - files taxes using an Employer Identification Number (EIN).

4. Recording and Automating Contractor Payments Accurately

QuickBooks offers flexible ways to record and even automate contractor payments:

1. Write a Check:

• Select the contractor, then click on Write Check.

• Select Bank account and enter the payment details, including amount, account category and description.

2. Create Expense or Bill

- Go to + New, then choose Check or Bill depending on how you pay your contractor.
- Select the contractor's name and enter the payment details, including account category and description.

3. Use Direct Deposit (with Payroll Add-On):

- If you're subscribed to QuickBooks Payroll, you can pay contractors via direct deposit—just like employees.
- Set up the contractor's bank info in their profile and schedule payments directly.

4. Recurring Payments (Optional):

- For ongoing work, you can make contractor payments recurring by saving the bill or expense as a recurring transaction.

5. Preparing and Filing 1099-NEC Forms for Tax Season

You don't withhold any taxes for 1099 contractors. That's their responsibility. But what you are responsible for:

- Filing Form 1099-NEC for each contractor paid $600 or more during the calendar year.
- Filing deadline is January 31, both to the IRS and to the contractor.

Here's how QuickBooks simplifies that process:

1. Select Contractor Accounts:

- Go to Payroll > Contractors > Prepare 1099s.
- Select accounts used to pay contractors and vendors, this is from your chart of accounts. The accounts can be expense accounts or banking accounts, depending on how you process and record contractor payments.

2. Review Recipents and Payment Totals

- QuickBooks Online displays the list of recipients who are tracked for 1099. Make sure you review the list to confirm all details before proceeding.
- Once the information is correct, click Next.

3. Preview the Finished Forms.

- QuickBooks Online will prepare the forms for your to review. Click the Preview button on each the recipient's name to review it.

4. E-File or Print and Mail:

- QuickBooks gives you option to e-file the forms directly with the IRS.
- You can also print copies for contractors and your records.

✓ Select accounts	2 **Review recipients**	3 Preview forms	4 File

Review recipients and payment totals

We pre-selected contractors and vendors you've been keeping track of for 1099s and who meet the IRS threshold for reportable payments in 2024. Review the list of folks you didn't track for 1099s to make sure no one was left out.

Why am I not seeing certain people or transactions?

Tracked for 1099   Not tracked for 1099

| Reportable payments only ⌄ | Total selected: 2 recipients |

	Name	Email	Address	TIN (EIN/SSN)	Reportable total ⓘ	Edit
☑	Mr Nathan Sparks	ngocmai.pham.ec@gmail.com	123 Street, AMK, CA 19793	XXX-XX-8977	$809.00	✏
☑	Mrs Emily Bond	emilybond@sample.com	123 Street, TMN, AK 12345	XXX-XX-9785	$908.00	✏

7171 ☐ VOID ☐ CORRECTED

PAYER'S name, street address, city or town, state or province, country, ZIP or foreign postal code, and telephone no. EverBloom Services		OMB No. 1545-0116	
		Form **1099-NEC** (Rev. January 2024) For calendar year **2024**	Nonemployee Compensation

PAYER'S TIN XX-XXX9875	RECIPIENT'S TIN XXX-XX-8977	1 Nonemployee compensation $ 809.00	**Copy A** For Internal Revenue Service Center
RECIPIENT'S name Mr Nathan Sparks		2 Payer made direct sales totaling $5,000 or more of consumer products to recipient for resale ☐	File with Form 1096.
		3	For Privacy Act and Paperwork Reduction Act Notice, see the current General Instructions for Certain Information Returns.
Street address (including apt. no.) 123 Street		4 Federal income tax withheld $	
City or town, state or province, country, and ZIP or foreign postal code AMK CA 19793		5 State tax withheld $	6 State/Payer's state no. CA	7 State income $ 809.00
Account number (see instructions)	2nd TIN not. ☐	$	

Form **1099-NEC** (Rev. 1-2024) Cat. No. 72590N www.irs.gov/Form1099NEC Department of the Treasury - Internal Revenue Service
Do Not Cut or Separate Forms on This Page — Do Not Cut or Separate Forms on This Page

---

5. Meet the Deadline:

- Be sure to file and send copies to contractors by January 31st of the following year.

With these tools and reminders in place, you'll be ready to handle 1099 filings like a seasoned pro. No confusion, no last-minute paperwork—just smooth, compliant contractor management.

Chapter 6: Inventory Management

I. Tracking and Managing Inventory

Effectively managing inventory is crucial for any product-based business. QuickBooks Online simplifies this process, providing real-time tracking and powerful reporting that eliminates uncertainty around stock levels, costs, and reorder timing. Let's examine how to utilize these tools efficiently and maintain full control of your inventory.

1. How QuickBooks Manages Your Inventory

QuickBooks Online uses a perpetual inventory system, updating stock quantities automatically whenever you purchase or sell items. This ensures constant accuracy in your records, enabling better insights into:

- Available stock levels
- Optimal reorder timing
- Accurate calculation of Cost of Goods Sold (COGS)
- Precise valuation of inventory assets

Note: Inventory tracking is available exclusively in QuickBooks Online Plus and Advanced subscriptions. Verify your plan includes inventory management capabilities before proceeding.

a. Inventory Asset Account: What You Own

When you purchase inventory items, QuickBooks records the cost as an increase to your Inventory Asset account—this is your current asset account that reflects the value of what's on your shelves. Each item's purchase price is stored in real-time, giving you visibility into how much you've invested in your stock.

This is a live number. As you sell products, the inventory quantity and its associated cost go down—automatically. You don't have to make manual journal entries unless you're correcting something. It's all done behind the scenes.

b. COGS: What It Cost You to Sell

Each time you sell an inventory item, QuickBooks calculates the cost of that item and moves it from your Inventory Asset account into your Cost of Goods Sold (COGS) account. This is the expense side of your inventory transaction, and it's what allows your Profit & Loss report to reflect true profitability.

For example, if you sell a floral arrangement for $100 and it cost you $40 in materials, QuickBooks will record $100 as income, and $40 as COGS—giving you a gross profit of $60. Simple, automatic, and accurate.

c. Understanding FIFO in QuickBooks Online

QuickBooks Online uses the FIFO (First In, First Out) method to calculate inventory costs. Here's what that means:

- FIFO assumes that the first inventory you purchase is the first to be sold.
- This affects how COGS is calculated—especially when purchase prices change over time.
- For example, if you bought roses at $2.00 per stem in January and again at $2.50 in March, sales will reflect the older (cheaper) inventory cost first.

This method is industry-standard and generally aligns with IRS regulations for small businesses. It's also particularly helpful when inventory costs fluctuate seasonally or due to supplier pricing changes.

d. Why This Matters

By understanding how QuickBooks tracks inventory:

- You'll know where your money is tied up.
- Your reports will show accurate gross profit margins.
- You'll be ready for better decision-making—whether it's pricing, purchasing, or planning.

In other words: set it up right, and let QuickBooks do the heavy lifting. It's one of the smartest moves you can make as a product-based business.

2. Inventory Types in QuickBooks

Knowing the difference between the item types in QuickBooks Online is essential to setting up your product and service list correctly. This isn't just a technical choice—it directly impacts how your books are maintained, how inventory is tracked, and what insights your reports will provide.

In chapter 3, we briefly mentioned about Item types in Products and Services. We will take a deeper look at these types in QuickBooks:

a. Inventory Items

These are physical products you buy, stock, and resell. QuickBooks will track quantities, costs, and inventory value automatically. When you use this type, QBO updates your Inventory Asset and COGS accounts with every transaction.

For example, with EverBloom Services sample company, we use this when:

- You sell floral arrangements, candles, or party supplies you keep in stock.
- You need to monitor how many units you have on hand.
- You want to track real-time inventory levels and costs.
- Example: "Rose Bouquet – Deluxe" with a quantity on hand of 25 units and a unit cost of $12.

b. Non-inventory Items

These are physical products you buy and sell but don't need to track quantities for. Maybe you purchase them for one-time use, or you custom-order them as needed.

Use this when:

- You don't want QuickBooks to track inventory levels.
- You sell made-to-order items or products you never physically store.
- You want simpler tracking for frequently purchased supplies.
- Example: "Custom Welcome Sign" for an event that's ordered on demand and never stocked.

c. Service Items

Service items are for non-tangible offerings like labor or consulting work. QuickBooks doesn't track quantities here—it's all about recording revenue for your time and expertise.

Use this when:

- You provide event planning, setup, or floral arrangement services.
- You charge by the hour, flat rate, or project.
- Example: "Event Coordination – Full Service" billed at $1,200 per event.

d. Bundles (Product/Service Bundles)

Bundles group multiple inventory, non-inventory, or service items together under a single product listing—great for streamlining sales and data entry.

Use this when:

- You frequently sell the same combination of items and services together.
- You want to simplify invoicing and save time.
- Example: A "Wedding Package" that includes 10 floral centerpieces

(inventory), setup service (service), and signage (non-inventory).

3. Properly Setting Up Your Inventory Items

Taking the time to set up your inventory items correctly from the start will save you countless hours down the road. In QuickBooks Online, good inventory setup isn't just about listing products—it's about tracking costs, maintaining clean records, and giving yourself the insights you need to make better business decisions.

Show Product/Service column on sales forms ⑦

Show SKU column ⑦

Turn on price rules ⑦

Track quantity and price/rate ⑦

Track inventory quantity on hand ⑦

Track inventory for sales channels

Revenue recognition ⑦ Learn more

Cancel   Save

Let's walk through the key elements of setting up an inventory item properly—and how each detail helps your financials stay accurate.

Name*
Plastic Roses

Item type
Inventory item   Add an image

SKU
PL-ROS

Category
Floral Supplies

Step 1: Enable Inventory Tracking

- Navigate to Settings (Gear icon) > Account and Settings.

- Select the Sales tab, go to Products and services section, then activate Track inventory quantity on hand.

Inventory info   ^

Initial quantity on hand*   As of date*   What's this as of date?
3,000   04/18/2025

Reorder point   What's the reorder point?   Inventory asset account*
450   Inventory Asset

Step 2: Add Inventory Items with Careful Details

- Click Sales & Get Paid > Products and Services, then select New.

- Choose Inventory as the item type.

- Enter essential product details clearly and thoroughly:

  » Name and SKU for easy identification.

  » Category for streamlined

Sales   ^

Description

Price/rate   Income account*
2   Sales of Product Income

Sales tax category   What's a sales tax category?
Taxable - standard rate

Purchasing   ^

Purchase description

Purchase cost   Expense account*
0.5   Cost of goods sold

Preferred vendor
Jessica Wong

reporting and analysis.

» Initial Quantity on Hand (the number of units you currently have in stock) and corresponding As of Date (the date QuickBooks starts tracking the item. Use the date of your opening balance or when you first take inventory).

» Reorder Point (the quantity at which QuickBooks will flag the item as low-stock - strongly recommended) to automate timely replenishment.

» Sales Price and Cost to ensure accurate margin analysis.

» Appropriate accounts for Income, Inventory Assets, and COGS.

Step 3: Review and Save

• Confirm all information, then click Save and Close.

A detailed setup from the beginning helps QuickBooks manage your inventory accurately and reduces future administrative adjustments.

4. Monitoring Inventory

One of the biggest headaches in inventory management is not knowing you're low—or completely out—of a product until it's too late. Whether you're prepping for an event or managing a storefront, timing is everything. QuickBooks Online gives you real-time visibility into your inventory so you can act before stockouts become a problem.

Products & services　　　　　🗭 Give feedback　　More ⌄　　New ⌄

> ⚠ Initial cost missing
> 7 items don't have an initial cost. Add now

> ❗ Low stock　　　　　　　　　　　　　×
> 1 item is running low on stock. See all

🔍 Search by name, SKU or category　　　Filter ⌄　　　　　　　🖨 🗗 ⚙

1-19 of 19　< 1 >

		NAME ⇕	QTY ON HAND ⇕	AVAIL QTY ⇕	CATEGORY ⇕	SKU ⇕	TYPE ⇕	PRICE ⇕	ACTION
⌐		Boutonniere & Cor...		0	Custom Products	CP-BOCO	Service	0	Edit | ⌄
⌐		Customized Bridal ...		0	Custom Products	CP-BRBQ	Service	0	Edit | ⌄
⌐		Decorative Vase	55	55	Floral Supplies	FS-VAS...	Inventory	0	Edit | ⌄
⌐		Delivery & Setup		0	Event Services	ES-DELIV	Service	0	Edit | ⌄
⌐		Event Consultation...		0	Event Services	ES-CONS	Service	0	Edit | ⌄
⌐		Event Planning - M...		0	Event Planning		Service	200	Edit | ⌄
⌐		Floral Arrangemen...		0	Event Services	ES-FLARR	Service	0	Edit | ⌄

a. Accessing the Products and Services List

Your hub for all things inventory is the Products and Services list:

- From the left-hand menu, click Sales & Get Paid > Products and Services.
- Here, you'll see every item you've created—inventory, non-inventory, services, and bundles.
- QuickBooks highlights inventory items that need your attention: low stock, out of stock, missing information.

b. Using the Quantity on Hand Dashboard

Think of the Quantity on Hand column as your "real-time pulse" on inventory.

- Positive numbers mean you're in the clear (for now).
- Zero means it's time to reorder—stat.
- Negative numbers? That's a red flag. Either a sale was recorded before receiving inventory, or there's a data entry error that needs correction.

Tip: Investigate negative quantities immediately. Letting them build up can lead to inaccurate COGS and overstatements in your inventory value—which could affect your financial reports and tax filings.

NAME ⬍	QTY ON HAND ⬍
Decorative Vase	60
Floral Foam (Box of 24)	30
Fresh Lilies (Dozen)	60
Fresh Roses (Dozen)	120
Fresh Tulips (Bunch)	80
Orchid Plant (Potted)	20
Plastic Roses	-200 **LOW** **OUT**
Satin Ribbons (Roll)	40
Seasonal Centerpiece	20

II. Creating and Managing Purchase Orders

Effective inventory management isn't just about monitoring existing stock—it also means efficiently handling incoming items. Purchase Orders (POs) in QuickBooks Online formalize your purchasing process, providing clarity and control over inventory acquisitions and vendor communication.

1. Why Use Purchase Orders?

A Purchase Order is a legally non-binding document that you send to a vendor to request goods or services. It outlines exactly what you're ordering—product details, quantities, costs, delivery dates—before anything is shipped.

In QuickBooks Online, a PO gives you internal visibility and control over your purchasing process. And even more importantly: it provides a paper trail in case something goes wrong.

a. Why Use Purchase Orders in QuickBooks Online?

- Internal Control and Accountability: Creating a PO sets clear expectations upfront—both for your team and your vendor. It ensures you're not over-ordering, duplicating requests, or forgetting what's already been ordered.

- Budgeting and Planning: POs can help you plan for future expenses and track commitments before bills arrive. They serve as a helpful preview of what's coming down the pipeline.

- Dispute Resolution: If you receive the wrong item, incorrect quantity, or get billed for something you didn't request, your PO becomes your best friend. It's a timestamped record of what was agreed upon.

- Inventory Coordination: With purchase orders enabled, you can monitor items on order (not yet received), helping you better forecast inventory needs and avoid stockouts or overstocking.

b. Purchase Orders vs. Bills: What's the Difference?

Feature	Purchase Order	Bill
Purpose	Request goods/services	Record what you owe after receiving
Timing	Before items are received	After items or services are delivered
Impact on Books	No financial impact	Increases accounts payable
Linked To	Vendor expectations	Payable and inventory accounts

2. Step-by-Step Guide to Creating a Purchase Order

Follow these clear steps to generate accurate, professional purchase orders in QuickBooks:

Step 1: Activate the Purchase Order Feature:

- Click the Gear icon and choose Account and Settings. Navigate to the Expenses tab, then toggle on Use purchase orders.
- Toggle on the Show Item table on expense and purchase forms.
- Click Save.

Step 2: Generate a New Purchase Order

- From the main menu, click + Create. Select Purchase order under the Vendors category.
- Alternatively, go to All Apps > Inventory > Purchase orders.

Step 3: Accurately Complete the Purchase Order

- Select your vendor from the list; QuickBooks automatically fills in their mailing address.
- Verify or update the shipping address, as needed.
- Clearly enter the PO date and note the expected delivery date if needed.
- Specify the products or services, ensuring accurate descriptions,

quantities, rates, and categories for straightforward tracking.

Step 4: Review, Save, and Send

Communicating clearly and promptly with vendors is critical:

- Select Save and Send to email your vendor a PDF copy of the purchase order instantly.
- Customize the accompanying email message as needed for clarity.
- QuickBooks automatically tracks when each PO is sent, simplifying your vendor communications records.
- Click Print or Preview within the PO to download or print as required.

Send email

To Cc/Bcc	priya@singhtech.com
	☐ Send me a copy
Subject	Purchase Order from EverBloom Services
Email body	Dear Priya Singh,
	Please find our purchase order attached to this email.
	Thank you
	EverBloom Services
	Manage online delivery settings

EverBloom Services

Purchase Order

VENDOR
Priya Singh
Singh Tech Solutions
890 Oakridge Way, Atlanta, GA 30303

SHIP TO
EverBloom Services

SERVICE   DESCRIPTION
Cost of goods
sold:Supplies & materials

SUBTOTAL
TOTAL

Cancel   Print   Send and close ∨

3. Effectively Tracking and Managing Outstanding Purchase Orders

Once you've sent a purchase order, your work isn't done—at least not yet. Staying on top of open and outstanding POs is essential to managing your cash flow, preventing stock delays, and keeping vendor relationships healthy.

QuickBooks Online gives you several ways to track open POs, so nothing falls through the cracks. Here's how to stay organized and proactive.

a. Viewing POs

When you're expecting inventory or materials, it's a good idea to check in on each vendor's outstanding orders. There are a few options to do this:

- Go to Expenses > Vendors: From the left-hand menu, click on Expenses, then choose Vendors. Click on the name of the vendor you're working with. You'll see a list of all transactions, including open purchase orders.

Aaron Patel ✉ ✎

Company	Billing address	Bill Pay ACH Info	SUMMARY
Patel Accounting LLC	1600 Walnut Street, Dallas, TX 75201	-	**$150.00** Open balance
Notes Add notes			**$0.00** Overdue payment

Transaction List   Vendor Details

All transactions ⌄   ⇄ Filter   Dates: Last 12 months

	DATE	TYPE	NO.	PAYEE	CATEGORY		TOTAL	APPROVAL STATUS	ACTION
☐	04/20/2025	Purchase Order	1003	Aaron Patel	Legal & accounting services	⌄	$250.00		View/Edit ⌄
☐	04/11/2025	Bill Payment	1	Aaron Patel			-$50.00		View/Edit ⌄
☐	04/11/2025	Bill	1001	Aaron Patel	Legal & accounting services	⌄	$200.00		Schedule payment ⌄

- Go to All Apps > Inventory > Purchase Orders: This gives you a view of all Purchase Orders and their statuses.

Purchase Orders   [Add purchase order]

Filters ⌄   Dates: Last 12 months

VENDOR	ORDER NO.	ORDER DATE	CATEGORY	CLASS	LOCATION	MEMO	TOTAL AMOUNT	STATUS		ACTION
Aaron Patel	1003	04/20/2025	Legal & accounting services				$250.00	Open		View/edit ⌄
Priya Singh	1002	04/20/2025	Supplies & materials				$600.00	Closed		View/edit ⌄
Michelle Turner	1001	04/20/2025	Inventory Asset				$1,500.00	Open		View/edit ⌄

- Go to Expenses > Vendors, then click on the Purchase Oder filter to view all open POs.

Vendors   ⓒ Give feedback   [Prepare 1099s ⌄]   [New Vendor ⌄]

$1,750.00 2 PURCHASE ORDER	Unbilled Last 365 Days	0 0. OVERDUE	Unpaid Last 365 Days	**$150.00** 1. OPEN BILLS	Paid	**$2,404.06** 10 PAID LAST 30 DAYS

Filter: [PURCHASE ORDERS] Clear filter / View all

Search 🔍

	VENDOR ↑	COMPANY NAME ⬍	PHONE	EMAIL	1099 TRACKING	OPEN PURCHASE ORDERS	PO AMOUNT ⬍	ACTION
☐	Aaron Patel	Patel Accounting LLC	(555) 456-7890	aaron@patelaccounting.com ✉		1 Open Purchase Order	$250.00	Create bill ⌄
☐	Michelle Turner	Turner Design Studio	(555) 246-8101	michelle@turnerstudio.com ✉		1 Open Purchase Order	$1,500.00	Create bill ⌄

Tip: You can also click into the PO itself to check details, send a follow-up email, or even convert it into a bill once the goods arrive.

b. Running Open Purchase Order Reports

To get the overview, run Open Purchase Order List report. It's a simple way to review everything that's been ordered but hasn't yet landed in your inventory.

1. Go to Reports > Standard Reports, search for Open Purchase Order List.
2. Customize as Needed: Filter by vendor, date range, or item type to zero in on what matters.
3. Export or Print: Share it with your purchasing team or keep it handy for weekly review meetings.

These reports help you manage vendor communications, plan cash outflows, and avoid surprises in your inventory.

c. Closing POs Manually (When Items Won't Be Received)

Sometimes, not every item gets delivered—and that's okay. But it's important to close out those POs so they don't clutter your reports. Here's how to manually close a PO:

1. Open the Purchase Order: Find it via the Vendor page or from your reports. Click the View/edit under the Action column.
2. Click the Drop-Down Next to the Status: If the PO won't be fulfilled (partially or fully), you can close it manually.
3. Select "Closed": Save your changes. The PO is now marked as closed and removed from open PO reports.

Open POs affect inventory expectations and financial planning. Keeping them accurate helps you stay grounded in what's actually coming and avoid false signals in your reorder process.

4. Recommendations and Best Practices:

- **Consistent PO Use:** Implement purchase orders consistently for all vendor orders, improving documentation and budget management.
- **Regular PO Reviews:** Frequently review open POs and follow up proactively with vendors to prevent supply delays.
- **Maintain Accurate Delivery Dates:** Clearly establish realistic expected delivery dates, allowing precise inventory planning and management.

By effectively leveraging QuickBooks Online's purchase order tools, you'll enhance your inventory management efficiency, prevent overspending, strengthen vendor relationships, and maintain accurate, audit-ready financial records.

III. Receiving Inventory and Managing Stock Levels

Effectively managing inventory means not only ordering the right items but also accurately receiving them and maintaining precise stock records. QuickBooks Online simplifies the entire process, from converting purchase orders into bills to making essential inventory adjustments, ensuring your business stays organized and profitable.

1. Receiving Inventory and Converting Purchase Orders into Bills

Once your ordered inventory arrives, it's critical to reflect this accurately in your financial records. Here's the best-practice method:

Step 1: Locate Your Purchase Order

- Follow the steps above to locate the relevant open purchase order.

Step 2: Convert the PO into a Bill

- Click View/edit to open the purchase order and click Copy to Bill.
- QuickBooks will automatically populate the bill with products, descriptions, and amount from the original PO.
- If it's a partial shipment, update amount to accurately reflect what you've physically received.
- Record additional charges such as shipping, handling, or other fees directly on the bill to ensure full cost accuracy.

Step 4: Finalize and Save the Bill

- Double-check your entries, then click Save and Close.
- Your inventory quantities automatically adjust, and accounts payable is accurately updated.

- If it is a partial shipment, QuickBooks will reflect a partial receipt, and the PO will remain open for the remaining items. In this case, you don't need to create a new PO—just repeat the process once the rest of the shipment arrives.

#	PRODUCT/SERVICE	DESCRIPTION	QTY	RATE	AMOUNT	RECEIVED	CLOSED	
1	Plastic Roses	1000 Plastic Roses	1000	1.50	$1,500.00	800		🗑
2								🗑

Add lines   Clear all lines

Total $1,500.00

Tip: Regularly reviewing and matching delivered items against POs promptly ensures accurate inventory counts and prevents billing discrepancies.

2. Adjusting Inventory Levels Manually

Even with the best systems in place, inventory records don't always align with what's physically on the shelves. That's where manual inventory adjustments come into play. Whether it's due to shrinkage, damage, counting errors, or regular audits, QuickBooks Online makes it easy to adjust quantities—but you'll want to do it with intention and proper accounting.

a. When to Use Inventory Quantity Adjustments

Here are a few common scenarios when an adjustment is necessary:

- You completed a physical inventory count and discovered a discrepancy.
- Products were damaged, spoiled, or otherwise unsellable.
- Items were stolen, lost, or miscounted previously.
- You need to write off obsolete inventory or reflect accurate year-end balances.

In short, if your quantity on hand in QuickBooks doesn't reflect the actual count, an adjustment is the cleanest way to reconcile it.

b. Making the Adjustment in QuickBooks

Step 1: Access the Inventory Adjustment Tool

- Click Sales & Get Paid > Products and Services.
- Locate the inventory item needing adjustment.
- Click the drop-down next to Edit and select Adjust quantity.

Step 2: Enter Adjustment Details

- Select the Adjustment Date (typically today or the end of a reporting period) and Adjustment Reason.
- Choose the Inventory Adjustment Account (more on that below).

- Enter the new quantity or the change in quantity.

🕐 Inventory quantity adjustment #10   ⑦

Adjustment date		Reference number
04/20/2025 📅		10

Adjustment reason		Inventory adjustment account ⑦
Damaged Goods ⌄		Inventory Shrinkage ⌄

#	PRODUCT/VARIANT	SKU	QTY ON HAND	NEW QTY	CHANGE IN QTY	
⠿ 1	Decorative Vase	FS·VASE01	60	55	-5	🗑

Step 3: Review and Record the Adjustment

- Verify accuracy before clicking Save and Close.
- QuickBooks updates your inventory automatically, providing clarity and precision in your financial reports.

c. Choosing the Correct Adjustment Account

If you create an inventory adjustment in QuickBooks, the software will automatically create an Inventory Shrinkage account after saving the adjustment. This is a default account where all the adjustments or changes you've made are recorded.

However, depending on your situation, you might want to create a few adjustment accounts for cleaner tracking and reporting. You can do this by creating a new account under Chart of Account.

Some common adjustment accounts you can create are:

- Spoilage or Damage: You may want a separate expense account if losses are due to breakage, expiration, or mishandling—especially in industries like food service or floral.
- Audit or Year-End Adjustments: If the discrepancy was found during a formal audit or year-end inventory review, consider creating a separate account like "Inventory Reconciliation Adjustments".

d. Best Practice:

- Document everything. Use the memo field to explain why the adjustment was made—especially if it's significant.
- Avoid using Cost of Goods Sold or general expense accounts directly: you want clear, auditable lines showing what happened and why.
- Make inventory adjustments immediately after discovering

discrepancies, as timely corrections significantly enhance the accuracy of your financial and inventory records.

3. Conducting Physical Inventory Counts and Reconciling

No matter how automated your inventory tracking may be, there's no substitute for physically counting what's actually in stock. Whether you're doing a full inventory count or a rotating cycle count, regular physical counts ensure your records are accurate—and help you catch problems before they become costly.

a. Best Practices for Cycle Counting

Cycle counting is a smarter, less disruptive alternative to shutting down operations for a full inventory sweep. Here's how to make it effective:

- Divide and conquer: Break your inventory into groups (by category, location, or value), and count a portion on a rotating basis—weekly, biweekly, or monthly.

- Count high-value or fast-moving items more frequently. These have the highest impact if they're off.

- Assign counting duties carefully. Choose team members who aren't responsible for ordering or receiving those items—this reduces the risk of bias or errors.

- Count at the same time of day. Try to avoid counting during busy restock or sales hours to minimize fluctuations.

b. Conduct Physical Count

Step 1: Prepare for the Physical Count

Physical Inventory Worksheet

Product/Service full name ⬦	Memo/Description ⬦	Quantity on hand ⬦	Reorder point ⬦	Quantity on PO ⬦
Floral Arrangements:Orchid Plan...	–	20.00	–	–
Floral Arrangements:Seasonal C...	–	20.00	–	–
Floral Foam (Box of 24)	–	30.00	–	–
Floral Supplies:Decorative Vase	–	55.00	–	–
Floral Supplies:Satin Ribbons (R...	–	40.00	–	–
Fresh Flowers:Fresh Lilies (Doz...	–	60.00	–	–
Fresh Flowers:Fresh Roses (Do...	–	120.00	–	–
Fresh Flowers:Fresh Tulips (Bun...	–	80.00	–	–
Plastic Roses	–	-200.00	450.00	–
TOTAL		**225.00**		**0.00**

- In QuickBooks, run the Physical Inventory Worksheet report (Reports > Standard Reports > search for Physical Inventory Worksheet).

- Print or export the report to PDF or Excel. This report lists all current items, SKUs, quantities on hand, and locations (if tracking is enabled), giving your team a clear checklist for counting.
- Arrange inventory logically to streamline counting and reduce errors.

Step 2: Execute the Physical Count

- Assign responsibilities clearly—ideally using two-person teams.
- Record actual inventory quantities directly on your worksheet.
- Pay special attention to high-value or high-turnover items, double-counting if necessary.

Step 3: Reconcile Physical Counts with QuickBooks Records

- Compare physical count totals against QuickBooks inventory records.
- For discrepancies, use the Adjust quantity feature, clearly documenting the reasons (e.g., damaged goods, errors, theft).
- Store all physical count worksheets as supporting documentation for audits or tax preparation.

IV. Inventory Reporting, Valuation & Insights

1. Inventory Valuation Reports

Inventory valuation reports in QuickBooks Online give you the clarity to make informed decisions about pricing, reordering, profitability, and tax prep. But it's important to understand exactly what these reports are showing you—especially when it comes to average cost versus unit cost.

a. Inventory Valuation Summary

Think of this as the high-level view. It lists each inventory item, the current quantity on hand, average cost, total asset value, and sales price, it is ideal for quick snapshots of what your inventory is worth and how much you've got in stock.

Use this report:

- Before preparing financial statements
- To review asset balances
- For board meetings and quick business checkups

b. Inventory Valuation Detail

This one gets into the weeds—and that's a good thing when you need answers. It shows every transaction that affects inventory quantity and value:

purchases, sales, adjustments, and returns. It breaks down how and when inventory values changed and what caused it.

Use this report:

Inventory Valuation Summary
EverBloom Services
As of April 20, 2025

Product/Service	SKU	Qty	Asset value	⇅ Calc. Avg
∨ Floral Arrangements				
Orchid Plant (Potted)	FA-ORCHP	5.00	75.00	15.00
Seasonal Centerpiece	FA-SEACEN	20.00	-	-
Total for Floral Arrangements	-	25.00	$75.00	-
Floral Foam (Box of 24)	FS-FOAM24	30.00	-	-
∨ Floral Supplies				
Decorative Vase	FS-VASE01	55.00	-	-
Satin Ribbons (Roll)	FS-RIB20	40.00	-	-
Total for Floral Supplies	-	95.00	-	-
∨ Fresh Flowers				
Fresh Lilies (Dozen)	FL-LIL12	60.00	-	-
Fresh Roses (Dozen)	FR-ROS12	120.00	-	-
Fresh Tulips (Bunch)	FT-TUL10	80.00	-	-
Total for Fresh Flowers	-	260.00	-	-
Plastic Roses	PL-ROS	300.00	450.00	1.50
TOTAL	-	**710.00**	**$525.00**	**$0.74**

- When investigating inventory discrepancies
- To audit historical changes in item cost
- For year-end inventory reconciliations

Inventory Valuation Detail
EverBloom Services
April 1-20, 2025

Product/Service ⇅	Transaction date ⇅	Transaction type	Num	Name	Qty	Rate ⇅	Inventory cost	Qty on hand	Asset value
> Floral Foam (Box of 24) (1)					30.00 (Total)		$0.00 (Total)		
∨ Plastic Roses (6)									
Plastic Roses	04/18/2025	Invoice	1010	City of Portland Parks & Rec	-2700.00	0.50	-1,350.00	-2700.00	-1,350.00
Plastic Roses	04/18/2025	Invoice	1011	Benson Hotel	-300.00	0.50	-150.00	-3000.00	-1,500.00
Plastic Roses	04/18/2025	Invoice	1011	Benson Hotel	-200.00	1.50	-300.00	-3200.00	-1,800.00
Plastic Roses	04/18/2025	Inventory Starting Value	START	-	3000.00	0.50	1,500.00	-200.00	-300.00
Plastic Roses	04/20/2025	Bill	-	Michelle Turner	800.00	1.50	1,200.00	600.00	900.00
Plastic Roses	04/20/2025	Invoice	1012	Benson Hotel	-300.00	1.50	-450.00	300.00	450.00
Total for Plastic Roses					300.00		$450.00		
> Floral Arrangements (2)					25.00 (Total)		$75.00 (Total)		
> Floral Supplies (2)					95.00 (Total)		$0.00 (Total)		
> Fresh Flowers (3)					260.00 (Total)		$0.00 (Total)		
					710.00		$525.00		

c. Sales by Product/Service Summary

Running a tight inventory system isn't just about knowing what you have. It's also about knowing what's moving. That's where the Sales by Product/Service

Summary report comes in. Here's what you can do with it:

Identify Top-Selling Items

- Quickly see which products are driving the most revenue.
- Easily spot top performers with high gross margin.
- Use this to decide what to promote, restock, or potentially bundle for more value.

Sales by Product/Service Summary
EverBloom Services
April 1-20, 2025

Product/Service	Quantity	Amount	% of sales	Avg. price	COGS	Gross margin	Gross margin %
-	-200.00	-40.00	-0.42 %	0.20	-	-	-
∨ Custom Products	0.00		0.0 %				
Customized Bridal Bouquet	1.00	80.00	0.85 %	80.00	-	-	-
Total for Custom Products	1.00	$80.00	0.85 %	$80.00	-	-	-
Event Planning - Mini Package	4.00	800.00	8.47 %	200.00	-	-	-
∨ Event Services	0.00		0.0 %				
Delivery & Setup	1.00	300.00	3.18 %	300.00	-	-	-
Floral Arrangement Service	1.00	150.00	1.59 %	150.00	-	-	-
Total for Event Services	2.00	$450.00	4.77 %	$225.00	-	-	-
∨ Floral Arrangements	0.00		0.0 %				
Orchid Plant (Potted)	25.00	1,000.00	10.59 %	40.00	475.00	525.00	52.5 %
Seasonal Centerpiece	5.00	300.00	3.18 %	60.00	-	-	-
Total for Floral Arrangements	30.00	$1,300.00	13.77 %	$43.33	$475.00	-	-
∨ Floral Supplies	0.00		0.0 %				
Decorative Vase	-10.00	-150.00	-1.59 %	15.00	-	-	-
Total for Floral Supplies	-10.00	-$150.00	-1.59 %	$15.00	-	-	-
TOTAL	3327.00	$9,440.00	100.0 %	$2.84	$2,725.00	-	-

Tip: Run this report regularly (monthly at a minimum) and compare it side-by-side with your Inventory Valuation Summary to tie movement to value.

d. Reconciling Inventory to General Ledger

Inventory reconciliation isn't just about matching what's on the shelf. It's also about making sure your Inventory Asset account on the balance sheet matches your Inventory Valuation Summary report in QuickBooks. This step is critical for clean financials and tax reporting.

Ensuring the Inventory Asset Balance Aligns

- Run Inventory Valuation Summary as of a specific date (month-end).
- Compare the total asset value to the balance of the Inventory Asset account in your chart of accounts on the Balance Sheet.

If they don't match? You may have:

- Incorrect product types (e.g., using non-inventory items when they should be inventory items)

- Manual journal entries affecting the Inventory Asset account (a big no-no unless you're fixing a specific error)
- Deleted or miscategorized transactions

Note: All inventory movement should flow through proper transactions (invoices, bills, inventory adjustments), never directly through journal entries.

Balance Sheet
EverBloom Services
As of April 20, 2025

Account	Total
∨ Assets	
∨ Current Assets	
> Bank Accounts	$658.22
> Accounts Receivable	$8,871.53
∨ Other Current Assets	
Inventory Asset	525.00
Payments to deposit	800.00
Total for Other Current Assets	$1,325.00
Total for Current Assets	$10,854.75
Fixed Assets	-
Other Assets	-
Total for Assets	$10,854.75

Finding and Fixing Imbalances

- Drill down into both the Inventory Valuation report and the Balance Sheet account.
- Look for transactions that bypass inventory workflows (e.g., using Expense instead of Inventory on a bill).
- Check for items mistakenly marked as non-inventory or services that should track quantity and value.

Once discrepancies are identified:

- Reclassify the transaction if it's posted incorrectly.
- Use inventory quantity adjustments (with notes) to correct counts or value.
- Consult your accountant before making manual adjustments to Inventory Asset—you don't want to break the audit trail.

By leveraging QuickBooks Online's inventory management tools thoughtfully, you can confidently manage your stock, minimize errors, and keep your focus on strategic business growth.

Chapter 7: Reporting and Analytics for Smart Decisions

I. Running Essential Financial Reports

Your financial data is far more than just numbers—it's the key to strategic decision-making, growth, and profitability. QuickBooks Online transforms transactions into actionable insights, empowering you to manage your business proactively. Let's explore the three essential reports every business owner must master: the Profit & Loss Statement, the Balance Sheet, and the Cash Flow Statement.

1. Understanding Your Profit & Loss Statement

Also called the Income Statement, the Profit and Loss (P&L) report gives you a clear snapshot of whether your business is making or losing money over a specific time frame. It's one of the first reports any lender, accountant, or investor will ask to see—and it should be one of your regular go-tos as well.

a. What does the P&L show?

- Revenue (or Income): How much money you've earned from sales of products or services.
- Cost of Goods Sold (COGS): The direct costs tied to those sales—think inventory, supplies, or labor if you're in a service business.
- Gross Profit: Revenue minus COGS. This tells you how much you're making before overhead.
- Operating Expenses: All your day-to-day costs—rent, software, utilities, marketing, and more.
- Net Profit (or Net Loss): What's left over after expenses. This is your true bottom line.

Tip: If you're consistently showing a net profit but struggling with cash flow, it's time to also run your cash flow report (we'll cover that next).

b. How to Run It in QuickBooks:

1. Go to the Reports tab from the left-hand menu, select Standard Reports.
2. By default, Profit and Loss is included in the Favorites section, click Profit and Loss report to run. Alternatively, you can find this report under the Business Overview section.
3. Choose your report period and accounting method—you can look at this month, last month, quarter-to-date, or custom dates.

∨ Favorites

Accounts receivable aging summary 📄 ★ ⋮

Balance Sheet 📄 ★ ⋮

Profit and Loss 📄 ★ ⋮

c. Customizing Your View: Using Display and Filter Tools

Use the Display by Feature: Need to break down your income and expenses by product, customer, employee, or location? Use the Display columns by dropdown to do just that.

- For example, if you run a floral and event planning business like EverBloom Services, displaying by Product/Service lets you see how each offering (e.g., event packages, corsages, or floral arrangements) contributes to your revenue and profitability.

- Displaying by Customer or Employee can help you identify your most valuable clients or the productivity of your team.

Refine with Filters: Once you've chosen how to view your report, you can zero in further using the Filter option. You can:

- Select specific products or services

- Filter by class, location, or customer

- Include or exclude certain accounts

- This allows you to build highly targeted reports—perfect for analyzing seasonal trends, tracking campaign results, or prepping for investor presentations.

Profit and Loss

EverBloom Services

January 1-April 22, 2025

Account	Event Planning - Mini Package	Orchid Plant (Potted)	Total for Floral Arrangements	Total
∨ Income				
Sales of Product Income	-	1,000.00	1,000.00	1,000.00
Services	800.00	-	-	880.00
Total for Income	800.00	1,000.00	1,000.00	$1,880.00
∨ Cost of Goods Sold				
Cost of goods sold	-	475.00	475.00	475.00
Total for Cost of Goods Sold	-	475.00	475.00	$475.00
Gross Profit	800.00	525.00	525.00	$1,405.00
Expenses	-	-	-	-
Net Operating Income	800.00	525.00	525.00	$1,405.00
Other Income	-	-	-	-
Other Expenses	-	-	-	-
Net Other Income	-	-	-	-
Net Income	800.00	525.00	525.00	$1,405.00

As you apply display and filter settings, the Profit & Loss report automatically refreshes to reflect your selections. The result? A focused financial view that's built for action, whether you're reviewing just a single product line or comparing performance across multiple services.

d. Compare Periods & Calculated Variances

Profit and Loss

EverBloom Services

January 1-April 22, 2025

Account	Jan 1 - Apr 22 2025	% of Expense	⟲ % of Income
	TOTAL		
∨ Income			
Discounts given	-40.00	-0.8 %	-0.37 %
Refunds to customers	-100.00	-1.99 %	-0.93 %
Sales	1,450.00	28.86 %	13.43 %
Sales of Product Income	8,150.00	162.24 %	75.5 %
Services	1,335.00	26.58 %	12.37 %
Total for Income	$10,795.00	214.89 %	100.0 %
∨ Cost of Goods Sold			
> Cost of goods sold	$2,925.00	58.23 %	27.1 %
Inventory Shrinkage	-	0.0 %	0.0 %
Total for Cost of Goods Sold	$2,925.00	58.23 %	27.1 %
Gross Profit	$7,870.00	156.66 %	72.9 %
> Expenses	$5,023.48	100.0 %	46.54 %
Net Operating Income	$2,846.52	56.66 %	26.37 %
Other Income	-	0.0 %	0.0 %
> Other Expenses	$199.06	3.96 %	1.84 %
Net Other Income	-$199.06	-3.96 %	-1.84 %

QuickBooks allows you to compare multiple time periods side-by-side:

- This year vs. previous year
- This period vs. previous period (e.g., comparing the first four months of 2025 with the last four months of 2024)
- This period vs. year-to-date
- This period vs. previous year-to-date
- Custom periods for analyzing seasonal trends

These comparisons help you understand what is happening and why.

When comparing Profit and Loss reports across different time periods, QuickBooks Online gives you the option to include calculated variances.

- $ change or % change: spot growth or declines between periods
- % of Row: calculates the row's value as a percentage of the row total

across time periods, great for seeing how each period contributes to the total for that row.

- % of Column: calculates each amount as a percentage of the column total.
- % of Expense: each line is shown as a percentage of total expenses. This is helpful for understanding which expenses take up the biggest slice of your budget.
- % of Income: shows each amount as a percentage of total income. This is commonly used for calculating profit margins or benchmarking costs against revenue.

These calculation tools turn your basic Profit and Loss report into a powerful analysis dashboard—no spreadsheets needed. Just click, compare, and make confident decisions!

e. Why It Matters:

The P&L isn't just for accountants. As a business owner, it shows you:

- If you're pricing products properly
- Whether overhead is creeping up
- If your marketing spend is returning value

By reviewing your Profit & Loss at least monthly, you'll build stronger financial instincts and make more confident decisions about where to save, invest, or pivot.

Tip: Consistently monitor your gross margin percentage and operating expense ratios. Doing so regularly allows you to proactively identify cost-saving measures and revenue-boosting opportunities before they become critical issues.

2. Navigating and Interpreting Your Balance Sheet

The Balance Sheet might not feel as flashy as a Profit & Loss report, but don't underestimate its importance—it's your business's financial snapshot at a specific point in time. While the P&L shows how your business is performing, the Balance Sheet shows what it owns, what it owes, and what's left over.

a. Key Sections to Know

- Assets – What your business owns. This includes:
  - » Current assets like bank balances, accounts receivable (money owed to you), and inventory.
  - » Fixed assets such as equipment, furniture, or vehicles.
- Liabilities – What your business owes. Common liabilities include:

» Accounts payable (vendor bills you haven't paid yet),

» Credit card balances, and

» Loans or lines of credit.

- Equity – What's left for you, the owner, after subtracting liabilities from assets. This includes owner's investment, retained earnings, and net income from the current year.

A healthy balance sheet shows that your business is growing its assets, managing its debts wisely, and building equity over time.

b. Accessing Your Balance Sheet:

- Navigate to Reports > Standard Reports and select Balance Sheet under the Favorites or Business Overview section.

Balance Sheet

EverBloom Services

As of April 22, 2025

Account	Total
∨ Assets	
∨ Current Assets	
> Bank Accounts	$658.22
> Accounts Receivable	$8,871.53
> Other Current Assets	$1,325.00
Total for Current Assets	$10,854.75
Fixed Assets	-
Other Assets	-
Total for Assets	$10,854.75
∨ Liabilities and Equity	
> Liabilities	$3,024.29
∨ Equity	
Retained Earnings	-1,717.00
Net Income	2,647.46
Opening balance equity	6,900.00
Total for Equity	$7,830.46
Total for Liabilities and Equity	$10,854.75

c. Customizing Your Balance Sheet with Display and Filter Options

QuickBooks Online doesn't just give you a standard balance sheet—it gives you a flexible tool to slice and dice your financial position in ways that matter most to your business. With the Display and Filter options, you can view your assets, liabilities, and equity from different angles—helping you uncover insights and spot anomalies in seconds.

Display by feature

Want to see how your financial position breaks down by product, store, or customer? Just use the Display columns by feature on the right-hand panel. For example, choose Customer to get a snapshot of how the balances align with specific clients.

Filter your data

Need a more focused view? The Filter option lets you zero in on specific vendors, customers, products or locations. This is especially handy when you have to reconcile a particular account or dig into a fluctuation in assets.

Display by	X		Filter ⑦	X
Select how you want to display columns.	Clear		Select how you want to filter your data.	Clear all
Display columns by			Product/Service ⌄	⊗
Customer ⌄			equals ⌄	
			Plastic Roses ⌄	

Balance Sheet

EverBloom Services

As of April 22, 2025

Account	Benson Hotel	City of Portland Parks & Rec	Not specified	⇕ Total
⌄ Assets				
› Current Assets	-900.00	-1,350.00	2,700.00	$450.00
Fixed Assets	-	-	-	-
Other Assets	-	-	-	-
Total for Assets	-900.00	-1,350.00	2,700.00	$450.00
⌄ Liabilities and Equity				
› Liabilities	-	-	-	-
⌄ Equity				
Retained Earnings	-	-	-	-
Net Income	700.00	4,050.00	-	4,750.00
Total for Equity	700.00	4,050.00	-	$4,750.00
Total for Liabilities ...	700.00	4,050.00	-	$4,750.00

Comparing Periods and Calculations

The Balance Sheet is a snapshot—it shows your business's financial position at a specific moment in time. While QuickBooks Online lets you compare Balance Sheets across different dates and even calculate percentages by row or column, these comparisons are more static than dynamic.

Unlike the Profit and Loss report, which tracks activity and trends over a period (like income growth or expense fluctuations), the Balance Sheet focuses on where your accounts stand—not how they got there. So while comparison tools exist, they're more useful for checking balances than uncovering deeper performance insights.

d. Why the Balance Sheet Matters to Lenders and Investors

If you ever apply for a loan or seek outside investment, this is one of the first reports a lender or investor will ask for. Why? Because it tells them:

- How leveraged your business is (how much debt you're carrying),
- Whether you have enough assets to cover your obligations, and
- Whether your business is increasing in value.

If your liabilities are climbing faster than your assets, it may signal cash flow concerns. If your equity is consistently growing, it tells a positive story of retained profits and solid financial management.

e. What to Watch Out For

- Negative Equity: This can be a red flag—meaning your business owes more than it owns.
- High Accounts Receivable (A/R): If customers aren't paying you on time, cash flow will suffer—even if your revenue looks great on the P&L.
- Unreconciled Balances: If something doesn't look right, click into the numbers. QuickBooks allows you to drill down to the transaction level.

Take time each month to review your Balance Sheet alongside your P&L and Cash Flow Statement. Together, they give you a full picture of your business's financial strength—and help you spot issues before they become problems.

f. Recommendations:

- Regularly confirm that all asset and liability balances reconcile to source documents.
- Drill down into accounts directly within QuickBooks to investigate any unusual or unexpected amounts immediately.
- Utilize QuickBooks' comparative balance sheets to analyze month-over-

month or year-over-year trends and identify significant shifts in your financial health.

Tip: Maintaining an accurate and well-organized balance sheet positions your business advantageously when seeking external funding, planning long-term investments, or preparing for tax reporting.

3. Utilizing Your Cash Flow Statement Effectively

When it comes to running a healthy business, cash flow is king. While your Profit and Loss report might show you're profitable, that doesn't always mean you have cash in the bank. That's where the Cash Flow Statement steps in—it tells the real story of what's coming in, what's going out, and what's left to work with.

QuickBooks Online's Statement of Cash Flows clearly illustrates how money enters and exits your business, providing valuable foresight to avoid cash shortages and maximize liquidity.

a. Accessing Your Cash Flow Statement:

- Select Reports > Standard Reports, then choose Statement of Cash Flows under Business Overview section.

	TOTAL
▾ OPERATING ACTIVITIES	
Net Income	2,647.46
▾ Adjustments to reconcile Net Income to Net Cash provided by operations:	
Accounts Receivable (A/R)	-8,871.53
Inventory Asset	-525.00
Accounts Payable (A/P)	1,700.00
Payroll Liabilities:Federal Taxes (941/943/944)	551.60
Payroll Liabilities:Federal Unemployment (940)	13.85
Payroll Liabilities:TN Quarterly Taxes	62.31
Tennessee Department of Revenue Payable	696.53
Total Adjustments to reconcile Net Income to Net Cash provided by operati...	-6,372.24
Net cash provided by operating activities	$ -3,724.78
▾ FINANCING ACTIVITIES	
Opening balance equity	6,900.00
Net cash provided by financing activities	$6,900.00
NET CASH INCREASE FOR PERIOD	$3,175.22
Cash at beginning of period	-1,717.00
CASH AT END OF PERIOD	$1,458.22

b. Editing the Cash Flow View

Customizing the Statement of Cash Flows Report in QuickBooks Online gives you a more focused view of how money moves through your business. You can choose to display columns by totals only or break it down by month, week, quarter, or year—perfect for spotting cash trends over time. You also have the option to display columns by Customer, Vendor, Store, or Product/Service to see exactly where cash is coming from or going.

On top of that, filters let you zero in on specific customers, vendors, stores, or products/services, helping you analyze cash flow sources and uses in a way that's highly actionable for your business.

	JAN - MAR, 2025	APR 1-22, 2025	TOTAL
▾ OPERATING ACTIVITIES			
Net Income	522.85	2,124.61	$2,647.46
▾ Adjustments to reconcile Net Income to Net ...			$0.00
Accounts Receivable (A/R)	-5.00	-8,866.53	$ -8,871.53
Inventory Asset		-525.00	$ -525.00
Accounts Payable (A/P)		1,700.00	$1,700.00
Payroll Liabilities:Federal Taxes (941/943/944)		551.60	$551.60
Payroll Liabilities:Federal Unemployment (9...		13.85	$13.85
Payroll Liabilities:TN Quarterly Taxes		62.31	$62.31
Tennessee Department of Revenue Payable		696.53	$696.53
Total Adjustments to reconcile Net Income t...	-5.00	-6,367.24	$ -6,372.24
Net cash provided by operating activities	$517.85	$ -4,242.63	$ -3,724.78
▾ FINANCING ACTIVITIES			
Opening balance equity		6,900.00	$6,900.00
Net cash provided by financing activities	$0.00	$6,900.00	$6,900.00
NET CASH INCREASE FOR PERIOD	$517.85	$2,657.37	$3,175.22

c. Cash In vs. Cash Out: The Real Story of Liquidity

QuickBooks Online's Statement of Cash Flows breaks your activity into three categories:

- Operating Activities: Includes daily income and expense transactions, like sales receipts and vendor payments—fundamental to assessing ongoing operational viability.
- Investing Activities: Highlights cash spent or received from asset acquisitions or sales, such as equipment purchases, property investments, or disposal of long-term assets.
- Financing Activities: Covers things like loan proceeds, repayments, and owner draws or contributions.

These sections help you see where your money is really moving—and whether you're cash-flow positive or negative.

d. Spotting Cash Flow Problems Early

Running short on cash doesn't usually happen all at once—it builds up slowly and quietly. By reviewing your cash flow regularly, you can:

- Catch trends early, like slowing customer payments or increasing expenses.
- See if your business is living beyond its means—even when sales look strong.
- Get ahead of problems by adjusting spending, invoicing sooner, or securing funding before things get tight.

QuickBooks also offers tools like the Cash Flow Planner to forecast upcoming inflows and outflows, helping you avoid surprises.

e. Plan for Big Purchases or Loan Applications

Thinking of buying new equipment? Hiring staff? Applying for a loan? Your Cash Flow Statement is your best friend.

- It shows lenders whether you can realistically handle debt.
- It shows if your timing is right—or if you need to build up reserves first.
- It even helps you set a realistic monthly reserve goal, so you're not caught off guard by seasonal slowdowns.

Consistent monitoring and forecasting of your cash flow enables proactive financial decision-making, avoiding expensive emergency borrowing, and helping maintain excellent vendor and banking relationships.

4. Understanding the Sales & Expense Reports

When you're running a business, it's not just about the big numbers like total revenue or net profit. It's about knowing the story behind those numbers— which products are flying off the shelves, which expenses are creeping up, and which customers or vendors are making the biggest impact. That's where the Sales and Expense reports in QuickBooks Online come in.

a. What Sales Reports Reveal (And Why They Matter)

Sales reports can be grouped in several ways—by customer, by product/ service, by store, or even by tag. Each lens tells a slightly different story. For instance:

- Sales by Customer Summary shows who your best customers are.
- Sales by Product/Service Detail reveals which offerings generate the most revenue.
- Estimates & Progress Invoicing Summary by Customer is incredibly helpful for businesses that work on long-term jobs or phased projects.
- Sales by Store or Sales by Customer Type is great if you operate across multiple locations or target different customer segments.

These reports help you focus your marketing, streamline your operations, and identify your strongest revenue streams. If you want to improve cash flow or set more realistic sales goals, these are the reports to start with.

Key Sales Reports to Prioritize

- Sales by Product/Service Detail – Understand what you're selling most.
- Sales by Customer Summary – Identify VIP customers and potential churn risks.
- Transaction List by Customer – Track down specific transactions quickly when questions arise.

Transaction List by Customer

EverBloom Services

April 1-23, 2025

Date ⌃	Transaction type ⌃	Posting (Y/N) ⌃	Account full name ⌃	Amount
⌄ Alder Creek Winery (5)				
04/10/2025	Invoice	Yes	Accounts Receivable (A/R)	87.40
04/10/2025	Sales Receipt	Yes	Cash	160.00
04/10/2025	Invoice	Yes	Accounts Receivable (A/R)	163.88
04/10/2025	Payment	Yes	Cash	110.00
04/11/2025	Credit Memo	Yes	Accounts Receivable (A/R)	-150.00
Total for Alder Creek Winery				$371.28
⌄ Benson Hotel (5)				
04/15/2025	Charge	No	Accounts Receivable (A/R)	200.00
04/15/2025	Credit	No	Accounts Receivable (A/R)	-200.00
04/18/2025	Invoice	Yes	Accounts Receivable (A/R)	1,092.50
04/20/2025	Invoice	Yes	Accounts Receivable (A/R)	655.50
04/20/2025	Invoice	Yes	Accounts Receivable (A/R)	1,000.00
Total for Benson Hotel				$2,748.00
⌄ City of Portland Parks & ... (1)				
04/18/2025	Invoice	Yes	Accounts Receivable (A/R)	5,899.50
Total for City of Portland Par...				$5,899.50
⌄ Lewis & Clark College (2)				

Tip: Compare seasonal trends to plan ahead for high-demand periods or promotional pushes.

b. What Expense Reports Tell You

On the flip side, expense reports help you see where your money is going— and where you might be able to cut back or renegotiate. Like sales reports, they can be grouped by vendor, by product/service purchased, or by store location. For example:

- Expenses by Vendor Summary shows which suppliers you spend the most with.
- Purchases by Product/Service Detail gives you insight into what's costing you the most—supplies, equipment, subcontractors, etc.

- Open Purchase Order Detail helps you stay on top of outstanding orders and budget commitments.

You can also look at Check Detail or Transaction List by Vendor to track individual payments and expenses when reconciling or preparing for tax season.

Essential Expense Reports to Review Regularly

- Expenses by Vendor Summary – Spot high-spending areas and negotiate where needed.

Expenses by Vendor Summary
January 1 - April 22, 2025

	TOTAL
Aaron Patel	200.00
David Kim	200.00
Emily Bond	1,000.00
Emily Carter	154.06
Internet	30.00
Nathan Sparks	900.00
Priya Singh	200.00
Not Specified	278.09
TOTAL	$2,962.15

- Purchases by Product/Service Detail – Know what you're buying most often and why.

Purchases by Product/Service Detail
EverBloom Services
April 1-23, 2025

Transaction date ⌄	Transaction type ⌄	Vendor ⌄	Line description ⌄	Quantity ⌄	Rate ⌄	Amount	Balance
⌄ Floral Foam (Box of 24) (1)							
04/09/2025	Inventory Starting Value	-	Floral Foam (Box of 24) - Openi...	30.00	-	0.00	0.00
Total for Floral Foam (Box of...				30.00		$0.00	
⌄ Plastic Roses (2)							
04/18/2025	Inventory Starting Value	-	Plastic Roses - Opening invent...	3000.00	0.50	1,500.00	1,500.00
04/20/2025	Bill	Michelle Turner	1000 Plastic Roses	800.00	1.50	1,200.00	2,700.00
Total for Plastic Roses				3800.00		$2,700.00	
⌄ Floral Arrangements (2)							
⌄ Orchid Plant (Potted) (2)							
04/09/2025	Inventory Starting Value	-	Orchid Plant (Potted) - Openin...	20.00	20.00	400.00	400.00
04/20/2025	Bill	Emily Carter	-	10.00	15.00	150.00	550.00
Total for Orchid Plant (Pott...				30.00		$550.00	
⌄ Seasonal Centerpiece (1)							
04/09/2025	Inventory Starting Value	-	Seasonal Centerpiece - Openin...	25.00	-	0.00	0.00
Total for Seasonal Centerp...				25.00		$0.00	
Total for Floral Arrangement...				55.00		$550.00	

- 1099 Transaction Detail Report – Ensure you're tracking payments properly for your contractors.

Watch for:

- Categories that are growing faster than revenue (a red flag)
- Monthly or quarterly spikes (could be subscription renewals, one-time purchases, or cost creep)
- Unexpected changes in vendor billing amounts

By reviewing your sales and expense reports regularly, you can spot trends early, avoid surprises, and plan with confidence. These aren't just compliance tools—they're strategic insights waiting to be used.

5. Running Accounts Receivable and Accounts Payable Reports

Your Accounts Receivable (A/R) and Accounts Payable (A/P) reports aren't just bookkeeping tools—they're your frontline insights for keeping your business financially healthy. They help you stay on top of incoming cash and outgoing obligations, so nothing gets missed, and your cash flow stays strong.

a. A/R Aging Summary: Who Still Owes You

A/R Aging Summary
As of April 22, 2025

	CURRENT	1 - 30	31 - 60	61 - 90	91 AND OVER	TOTAL
Amy's Bird Sanctuary		239.00				$239.00
Bill's Windsurf Shop			85.00			$85.00
▾ Freeman Sporting Goods						$0.00
0969 Ocean View Road	477.50					$477.50
55 Twin Lane		4.00	81.00			$85.00
Total Freeman Sporting Goods	477.50	4.00	81.00			$562.50
Geeta Kalapatapu	629.10					$629.10
Jeff's Jalopies		81.00				$81.00
John Melton		450.00				$450.00
Kookies by Kathy			75.00			$75.00
Mark Cho	314.28					$314.28
Paulsen Medical Supplies	954.75					$954.75
Red Rock Diner	70.00			156.00		$226.00
Rondonuwu Fruit and Vegi	78.60					$78.60
▸ Shara Barnett		274.50				$274.50
Sonnenschein Family Store	362.07					$362.07
Sushi by Katsuyuki	80.00	80.00				$160.00
Travis Waldron	414.72					$414.72
Weiskopf Consulting	375.00					$375.00
TOTAL	$3,756.02	$1,128.50	$241.00	$156.00	$0.00	$5,281.52

The Accounts Receivable Aging Summary shows your outstanding customer balances organized by how long they've been unpaid—think 0-30 days, 31-60 days, and so on. Here's what to look for:

- Current balances: Great! These are on track.
- 30+ days overdue: Time for a follow-up.
- 60+ days overdue: These may need collection strategies.

Tip: Click on any amount to see the original invoice, email history, and even resend it directly.

What to do with overdue balances:

- Send friendly reminders or statements.
- Offer a small discount for quick payment if it makes sense.
- Reach out personally—sometimes a quick phone call works wonders.

To improve your cash flow, you want your A/R report to stay lean. Try these smart strategies:

- Send invoices promptly after delivering a product or service.
- Set up automatic reminders in QuickBooks so customers don't forget.
- Accept online payments—it shortens the turnaround time.
- Review the A/R report weekly so you're always on top of it.

b. A/P Aging Summary: What You Owe

A/P Aging Summary
As of April 22, 2025

	CURRENT	1 - 30	31 - 60	61 - 90	91 AND OVER	TOTAL
Brosnahan Insurance Agency		241.23				$241.23
Diego's Road Warrior Bodyshop	755.00					$755.00
Norton Lumber and Building Mat...		205.00				$205.00
PG&E			86.44			$86.44
Robertson & Associates		315.00				$315.00
TOTAL	$755.00	$761.23	$86.44	$0.00	$0.00	$1,602.67

The Accounts Payable Aging Summary works the same way—except it's showing your unpaid vendor bills. It's a fantastic tool for:

- Avoiding late fees
- Prioritizing payments by due date or vendor importance
- Managing vendor relationships with confidence

Prioritize your vendor payments by:

- Paying time-sensitive bills first (especially ones with penalties)
- Leveraging payment terms (like Net 30 or Net 60)

- Holding off on non-essential payments if cash is tight

When you stay plugged into your A/R and A/P reports, you're not just reacting—you're taking control. That means fewer surprises, stronger vendor relationships, and a healthier bank balance.

II. Customizing Reports for Strategic Insights

QuickBooks Online's default reports are powerful on their own, but the true value emerges when you tailor them specifically to your business needs. Customized reporting enables deeper analysis, clearer communication with stakeholders, and smarter strategic decision-making. Let's explore how you can effectively select, customize, save, and analyze your reports for maximum business impact.

1. Selecting and Tailoring Report Templates

Start by choosing a base template, then modify it to highlight exactly the details you need:

Step 1: Choose the Right Base Report

Navigate to Reports from the left-hand menu and select a report that aligns with your goal. Popular starting points include:

- Profit and Loss – for financial performance
- Sales by Customer or Product – to track revenue sources
- Expenses by Vendor – for budget or cost control analysis

Step 2: Customize for Business Insights

- Click Customize in the top right of your selected report. Instead of general display or filter tools (which we covered in Section 1), now think strategically:
  » Compare time periods (month vs. month, this year vs. last) to identify trends.
  » Group by categories that matter, such as Class, Location, or Department (if enabled).
  » Add calculation columns—like % of income or % change—to highlight relationships and shifts in performance.
  » Organize your columns to bring the most important figures front and center.

Step 3: Drill Down and Validate

Once you click or hit Run Report, don't stop at the numbers. Click into them to drill down and investigate:

- Large variances from one period to the next
- Unexpected expenses
- High-performing products or regions

This is where real analysis happens.

Sales by Customer by month by Product 1

Customer	January 2025	February 2025	March 2025	≎ Total
Amy's Bird Sanctuary	-	-	275.00	275.00
Cool Cars	-	-	400.00	400.00
Dukes Basketball Camp	-	422.00	-	422.00
Dylan Sollfrank	-	-	337.50	337.50
> Freeman Sporting Goods	275.00	-	290.00	$565.00
Geeta Kalapatapu	-	-	582.50	582.50
John Melton	-	-	750.00	750.00
Kate Whelan	-	-	225.00	225.00
Mark Cho	-	-	275.00	275.00
Paulsen Medical Supplies	-	-	755.00	755.00
Red Rock Diner	48.00	-	-	48.00
Rondonuwu Fruit and Vegi	-	-	45.00	45.00
> Shara Barnett	-	-	275.00	$275.00
Sonnenschein Family Store	-	-	335.25	335.25
Travis Waldron	-	-	187.55	187.55
Weiskopf Consulting	-	-	375.00	375.00
TOTAL	**323.00**	**422.00**	**5,107.80**	**$5,852.80**

Tip: Customize frequently accessed reports to streamline your regular review processes, saving you time and ensuring consistent reporting standards.

2. Saving and Automating Customized Reports

No need to repeat your work every month. Once your report is just right, QuickBooks helps you lock it in and automate delivery.

Step 1: Save the Custom Report

Click Save Customization and give your report a clear, functional name like:

Save as new report?

Changes will be saved to the new report. This report will remain unchanged.

Report name

Sales by Customer by month by Produc

Share with others

This report is only visible to you.

Add to group (optional)

Select

Cancel   Save

- "Monthly Sales by Product – West Region"
- "Board P&L – YoY Comparison"

Step 2: Reuse Easily

Go to Reports > Custom Reports to revisit or update any saved version—no need to recreate from scratch.

Step 3: Automate Delivery

Click on the drop-down button in the Action column, then choose Create a schedule:

- Set the start date, end date and frequency—weekly, monthly, quarterly
- Add your recipients whom will receive the report via emails
- Add a message so stakeholders know what to look for

Create and send recurring report

| Start | 05/01/2025 | at | 9:00am |
| | Asia/Bangkok | | |

| Repeat every | 1 | Month |

- (●) 1 of the month
- ( ) Fourth Wednesday of the month

| End | (●) 12/31/2025 |
| | ( ) Never |

How would you like this action to happen?

☑ Send a company email

Send to

| markbenson@everbloom.com | Add CC | Add BCC |

Subject

This turns your reports into living tools, not static documents. Everyone stays informed—automatically.

Recommendation: Scheduling automated reports ensures consistency and timeliness, keeping your management team informed proactively without the hassle of manual distribution.

3. Analyzing Data for Actionable Insights

Custom reports aren't just for viewing; they're critical tools for strategic decision-making. Here's how you can leverage them effectively:

- Identify Trends: Regularly assess patterns, such as sales growth in specific areas, increasing expenses, or shifting customer preferences.
- Perform Comparative Analysis: Use comparison features within QuickBooks (such as month-over-month, quarter-over-quarter, or year-over-year views) to detect anomalies, seasonal cycles, or long-term trends.
- Drive Strategic Decisions:
  » If particular products or services underperform, consider strategic adjustments—pricing revisions, targeted marketing, or potential discontinuation.
  » Identify highly profitable customers or segments and increase resources dedicated to retaining and expanding these relationships.
- Facilitate Team Collaboration: Share critical insights regularly with finance teams, marketing departments, or operational managers, ensuring everyone aligns around informed business decisions.

Recommendation: Transform data into actionable strategies by discussing customized reports routinely in management meetings, quarterly reviews, or strategic planning sessions. This practice embeds data-driven decision-making deeply into your business culture.

III. Forecasting and Budgeting for Growth

Successful businesses don't just react—they plan ahead strategically. QuickBooks Plus and Advanced plans offer tools that can give you a proactive approach to managing finances, anticipating growth opportunities, and steering your business with clarity and confidence. Here's how you can effectively use these tools to shape a healthy financial future.

1. Creating Budgets in QuickBooks Online

A well-prepared budget is your roadmap to financial discipline, guiding spending decisions, pinpointing areas of concern early, and helping you achieve clearly defined financial goals.

Step 1: Access the Budgeting Feature

- Click the Gear icon (top right corner), then select Budgeting under Tools. Alternatively, you can select Reports > Financial Planning on the left panel, and select Budgets.
- Click on Create budget to begin setting up your budget.

Step 2: Define Your Budget Parameters

How do you want to set up your budget?

Select your preferred options

Budget type   ⦿ Profit and loss ⓘ   ◯ Balance sheet ⓘ

Period | FY 2026 (Jan 2026 - Dec 2026) ⌄ |

Budget format   ⦿ Consolidated ⓘ   ◯ Subdivided ⓘ

Pre-fill data | Actuals 2025 (YTD) ⌄ | **Clear**

Available setup option

◯ △
◇ ☐

Custom budgets
Create a budget from scratch

Create budget in spreadsheet ⑦

- Select the budget type: Profit and Loss or Balance Sheet. In practice, most businesses start with Profit and Loss, then work their way toward Balance Sheet (if needed). For small businesses, budgeting for Balance Sheet is just a cherry on top.
- Select the appropriate period for your budget (e.g., 2026).

- Select the budget format consolidated or subdivided. Subdivided budget is useful when your company has significant locations, sales centers or departments where separate budgets make sense. Otherwise, a consolidated budget is generally enough.
- If you have historical data, always select Pre-fill data, unless you are changing the business model or your business approach and strategy, where a zero-based budgeting can be best suitable.
- Click Next to start budgeting.

Step 3: Input Your Budget Figures

- For each income and expense account, input your anticipated monthly amounts.
- To simplify the process, start by copying prior year actual figures, then adjust based on your strategic goals or market expectations.

Period				Reference data							
FY 2026 (Jan 2026 - Dec 2026)		Compare reference data ⬤		Actuals 2025 (YTD)		Yearly ∨	Quarterly	Monthly			
Batch actions ∨ ⓘ 🔍 Find by account name or numb						🔗 Autosave on	Show all reference data	Export/Print ∨	⚙		
☐ ∧ **Accounts**	Actuals 2025 (YTD)	◀ Budget totals	▶	Jul 2026 ▶	Aug 2026 ▶	Sep 2026 ▶	Oct 2026 ▶	Nov 2026 ▶	Dec 2026		
☐ ∧ **Income**											
☐ Billable Expense Income	0.00										
☐ Discounts given	-40.00	-40.00		0.00	0.00	0.00	0.00	0.00	0.00		
☐ Event Planning Revenue	0.00										
☐ Refunds to customers	-100.00	-100.00		0.00	0.00	0.00	0.00	0.00	0.00		
☐ Sales	1,450.00	1,450.00		0.00	0.00	0.00	0.00	0.00	0.00		
☐ Sales of Product Income	8,150.00	8,150.00		0.00	0.00	0.00	0.00	0.00	0.00		
☐ Services	1,335.00	1,335.00		0.00	0.00	0.00	0.00	0.00	0.00		
☐ Unapplied Cash Paymen...	0.00										
☐ Uncategorized Income	0.00										
Total Income	10,795.00	10,795.00		0.00	0.00	0.00	0.00	0.00	0.00		

Step 4: Save and Activate Your Budget

- Click Save and Close once your budget entries are complete.

Tip: When developing your budget, avoid overly optimistic or pessimistic projections. Strive for realistic numbers—based on historical performance, adjusted for anticipated changes—this ensures the budget remains both achievable and meaningful.

2. Tracking Budget vs. Actual Performance

Creating a budget is just the first step. Regularly comparing your planned figures to actual results is essential to maintain financial control and adaptability.

Step 1: Generate Your Budget vs. Actual Report

- Navigate to Reports > Standard Reports > Budget vs. Actual.
- Select the budget you created and the desired reporting period.

Step 2: Analyze and Understand Variances

- Identify significant deviations between actual performance and your budget.
- Pay close attention to recurring discrepancies—are certain expenses consistently over budget? Are revenues consistently falling short?

EverBloom Services ✏️

Budget vs. Actuals: Budget_FY25_P&L - FY25 P&L
April 2025

	APR 2025			
	ACTUAL	**BUDGET**	**OVER BUDGET**	**% OF BUDGET**
▾ Income				
Billable Expense Income		10,000.00	-10,000.00	
Discounts given	-40.00	-100.00	60.00	40.00 %
Event Planning Revenue		2,083.33	-2,083.33	
Refunds to customers		0.00	0.00	
Sales	500.00	1,208.33	-708.33	41.38 %
Sales of Product Income	8,150.00	20,833.33	-12,683.33	39.12 %
Services	1,330.00	2,779.17	-1,449.17	47.86 %
Total Income	$9,940.00	$36,804.16	$ -26,864.16	27.01 %
▾ Cost of Goods Sold				
▸ Cost of goods sold	2,925.00	6,475.00	-3,550.00	45.17 %
Inventory Shrinkage	0.00	833.33	-833.33	0.00 %
Total Cost of Goods Sold	$2,925.00	$7,308.33	$ -4,383.33	40.02 %
GROSS PROFIT	$7,015.00	$29,495.83	$ -22,480.83	23.78 %
▸ Expenses	$4,890.39	$14,657.06	$ -9,766.67	33.37 %
NET OPERATING INCOME	$2,124.61	$14,838.77	$ -12,714.16	14.32 %
▸ Other Expenses	$0.00	$0.00	$0.00	0.00%
NET OTHER INCOME	$0.00	$0.00	$0.00	0.00%
NET INCOME	$2,124.61	$14,838.77	$ -12,714.16	14.32 %

Step 3: Adjust and Refine Your Approach

- If expenses exceed budget, proactively consider cost reduction strategies or tighter spending controls.
- When revenue targets are missed, revisit sales and marketing plans, adjusting strategies to improve performance.

Recommendation: Review your budget-vs-actual report monthly, using it as a key discussion point in management meetings. Early and frequent reviews help quickly identify issues, allowing prompt action before minor variances become major financial headaches.

3. Forecasting Revenue and Expenses

Effective forecasting is about leveraging past performance and market insights to anticipate future outcomes. This proactive approach can help your business capitalize on opportunities and mitigate potential challenges.

Set up your forecast

Choose how you want to set up your profit and loss forecast. View projections for up to 3 years. Find out more

Forecast for	Rest of the year (Apr 2025 - Dec 2025) ⌄
Forecast using	Average of actuals ⌄
	See how this works
Use actuals from	Last 3 months ⌄

Set rules (optional) ⓘ

Income accounts	Increase ⌄	by	40 %	Clear
COGS accounts	Increase ⌄	by	10 %	Clear
Expense accounts	Increase ⌄	by	10 %	Clear
Other Income accounts	Increase ⌄	by	10 %	Clear
Other Expense accounts	Decrease ⌄	by	30 %	Clear

Step 1: Identify Historical Trends

- Analyze past Profit and Loss statements, reviewing monthly or quarterly figures.

- Look for patterns in revenues, expenses, and profitability—pay particular attention to seasonality, growth cycles, and recurring financial events.

Step 2: Build a Practical Forecast

- Navigate to Financial Planning > Forecasts, click Create forecast.
- Start with recent historical data, then apply adjustments based on strategic changes—like planned price increases, new product launches, or shifts in marketing investment. Click Next to continue.
- QuickBooks Online will base on your assumptions to create a simple forecast. You can review and edit each number manually if you have more information.

Forecast_P&L (Apr 2025 - Dec 2025) ✎

Batch Actions ∨ ⓘ

∧ Accounts	Jan 2025 Actuals	Feb 2025 Actuals	Mar 2025 Actuals	Apr 2025 Forecast	May 2025 Forecast	Jun 2025 Forecast
∧ Income						
☐ Billable Expense Income	0	0	0			
☐ Discounts given	0	0	0			
☐ Event Planning Revenue	0	0	0			
☐ Refunds to customers	0	0	-100	-47	-62	-83
☐ Sales	0	0	950	443.33	9000 ⊖	788.15
☐ Sales of Product Income	0	0	0			
☐ Services	0	0	5	2	3	4
☐ Unapplied Cash Paymen...	0	0	0			
☐ Uncategorized Income	0	0	0			
Total Income	**0**	**0**	**855**	**399**	**8,941**	**709**
∧ Cost of Goods Sold						
☐ ∧ Cost of goods sold	0	0	0			
☐ Equipment rental	0	0	0			
☐ Subcontractor expenses	0	0	0			
☐ Supplies & materials	0	0	0			
Total Cost of goods sold	**0**	**0**	**0**	**0**	**0**	**0**

Step 3: Regularly Review and Update

- Forecasts should never be static. Adjust your forecasts quarterly or whenever significant business changes occur.
- Use revised forecasts to inform key business decisions such as hiring, equipment investments, or securing financing.

Tip: Treat forecasting as a strategic, ongoing process—not a one-time task. Regular forecast updates ensure your business remains agile, resilient, and strategically aligned with your growth objectives.

IV. Using Audit Logs to Protect Your Data Integrity

As an experienced accountant, I can't emphasize enough how critical accurate and trustworthy financial records are for your business. QuickBooks Online's built-in Audit Log provides robust transparency, keeping a detailed record of every activity—who made the change, exactly what was changed, and precisely when. Think of the audit log as your internal safeguard, ensuring accountability, security, and data integrity. Here's how to use it effectively.

1. Accessing and Reviewing the Audit Log

Regularly checking your audit log can be a lifesaver, especially during audits, tax season, or when investigating discrepancies.

Step 1: Open Your Audit Log

- Click the Gear icon (top-right corner).
- Select Audit Log from the Tools menu.

DATE CHANGED ↓	USER	EVENT	HISTORY
Apr 23, 2025, 9:24 pm	Craig Carlson	Edited user Craig Carlson	View
Apr 23, 2025, 3:11 pm	Craig Carlson	Signed Out.	
Apr 23, 2025, 3:07 pm	Craig Carlson	Signed In.	
Apr 23, 2025, 7:56 am	System Administration	Changed settings	
Apr 23, 2025, 7:56 am	System Administration	Changed settings	
Apr 23, 2025, 7:56 am	Craig Carlson	Edited Timesheet to Emily Platt	View
Apr 23, 2025, 7:56 am	Craig Carlson	Edited Timesheet to Emily Platt	View

Step 2: Narrow Your View with Filters

- Quickly filter by:
  - » User: Review actions by specific team members.
  - » Date range: Select a custom period to pinpoint activities.
  - » Event type: Choose specific actions—created, edited, deleted transactions, login events, etc.

Step 3: Examine Entries in Detail

- Each entry shows clearly who made the change, when, and what specifically changed.
- Click View next to any suspicious or unclear entry for comprehensive details, including the before-and-after values.

Tip: Routinely review the audit log—monthly or quarterly. Regular checks simplify identifying irregularities or mistakes, allowing timely correction before minor issues escalate.

2. Detecting and Investigating Unusual Activity

Vigilance is key to catching errors or unauthorized changes. Here's how you can leverage the audit log to protect your financial data:

- Identify Red Flags Promptly:
  » Look for deleted or significantly edited transactions, especially income, expense, or payroll entries.
  » Be alert to user activity at unusual hours or atypical user actions (e.g., sales personnel altering vendor bills).
- Investigate Thoroughly:
  » Drill down on suspicious changes to evaluate whether they're genuine errors, malicious actions, or misunderstandings.
  » Cross-reference other actions taken by the user to understand the scope.
- Address Issues Directly:
  » Promptly clarify unusual changes directly with involved team members.
  » Restore correct information, make adjusting entries, and document your review process clearly.

Recommendation: Combine audit log reviews with periodic reconciliations and financial analyses. A holistic approach enhances your ability to spot anomalies early, protecting your business from financial inaccuracies or fraud.

3. Best Practices for Maintaining Data Security

The integrity of your data doesn't just rely on QuickBooks; it depends significantly on how you and your team use it. Implement these best practices to fortify your data security:

- Define and Manage User Access Carefully:

- » Navigate to Gear icon > Manage Users to ensure each user has appropriate permissions.
- » Limit sensitive access—such as payroll, bank feeds, or vendor payments—to trusted senior team members.

- Strengthen Login Security:
- » Mandate strong, unique passwords for all users.
- » Activate two-factor authentication (2FA) to add an essential security layer.

- Establish Routine Audit Log Reviews:
- » Schedule regular audit log checks into your monthly or quarterly routine.
- » Document and store findings securely to support accountability and future audits.

- Educate and Engage Your Team:
- » Conduct regular QuickBooks and security best practices training.
- » Explain clearly that audit logs are essential tools for maintaining accuracy and trust—not for micromanaging or controlling your team.

Tip: Remember, your audit log is more than just a compliance measure. It's a valuable tool that fosters accountability, ensures your financial integrity, and builds a culture of transparency and trust within your organization.

Chapter 8: Advanced Features and Workflow Automation

I. Managing Projects in QuickBooks Online

If your business juggles multiple jobs, client projects, or events at once, QuickBooks Online Projects can be a game-changer. It gives you a dedicated space to track income, expenses, and time—so you can stay on top of job profitability without bouncing between spreadsheets or manually adding things up.

Let's break down how to use this feature to its full potential.

1. What the Projects Feature Is (and Isn't)

Projects in QuickBooks Online are designed for job-costing—which means tracking all income and expenses related to a specific job, client, or event.

Great use cases for Projects include:

- A floral and event planning business managing separate weddings or corporate events
- A contractor handling multiple remodeling jobs for different clients
- A freelancer organizing income and billable hours by client

When NOT to use Projects:

- For simple, unrelated sales (like one-off product sales with no associated job costs)
- If you only need general reports by customer (using the Customer center is enough)
- When you don't track income/expenses separately by job

Projects work best when there's a clear beginning and end, a defined budget or scope, and expenses tied directly to that project.

2. Setting Up a New Project

Let's get you rolling with your first project:

Projects   Organize all job-related activity in one place ⑦

Cancel   Save

1. Turn On Projects (if it's not already active):
   » Go to the Gear icon > Account and Settings > Advanced > Projects
   » Turn it ON and click Save.

2. Create a New Project:
   » Head to All Apps > Projects in the left-hand menu.
   » Click New Project and give it a name (e.g., "Wedding Lisa & Jordan").
   » Assign the project to a customer or sub-customer.
   » Add start date and end date of the project.
   » Add notes or details if needed, then click Save.

3. Start Linking Transactions:

From the Project Dashboard, click Add to Project and choose what you want to enter:

- Invoices or payments for services or products sold
- Expenses or bills for supplies, rentals, or subcontractors
- Time entries for employees or contractors
- Estimates, purchase orders, or journal entries

Every transaction tagged to this project will feed into its financial overview, keeping everything nice and neat.

3. Tracking Profitability by Project

Once your transactions are rolling in, this is where Projects starts to shine.

From the Project Dashboard, you'll get a real-time look at:

- Income: Invoices and sales receipts tied to the project
- Costs: All bills, expenses, time costs, and checks
- Profit Margin: The difference between the two

See info based on

| Payroll Expenses ∨ |

Project balance summary

INCOME	COSTS	PROFIT
$600.00	**$150.00**	**$450.00**
Actual $600.00 — Estimated $2,000.00	Actual $150.00 — Estimated $2,000.00	Actual profit margin 75.00%
View details	View details	

$655.50
Open invoices
View all

$0.00
Overdue invoices
View all

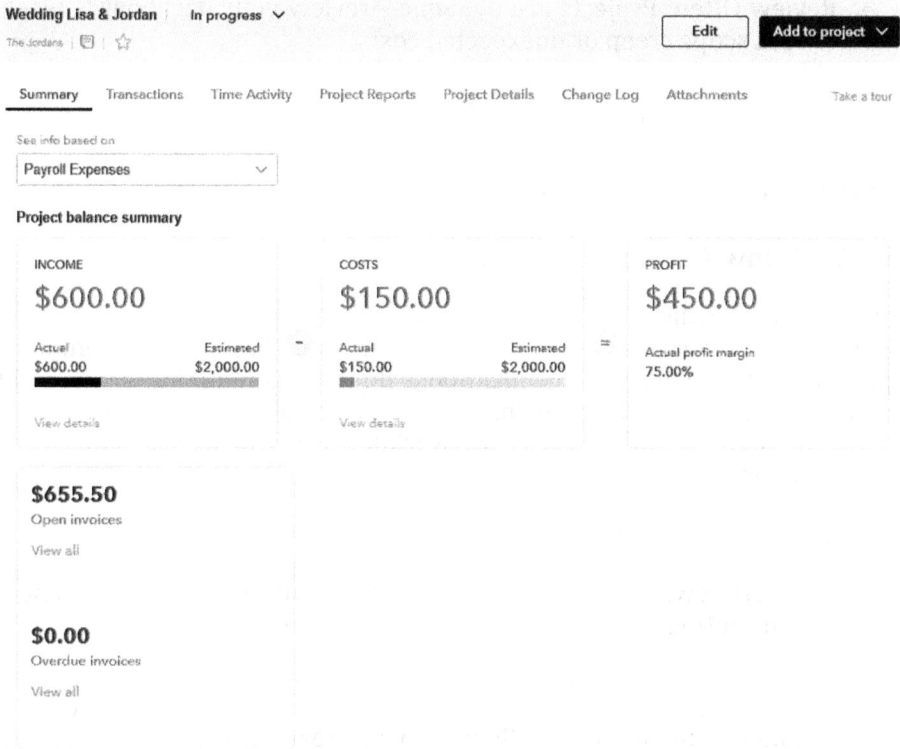

You can also run detailed reports like:

- Project Profitability – Total income vs. total costs by project
- Time cost by employee or vendor – Time tracked, hourly cost rates, and gross profit per employee or vendor.

Use these insights to adjust your pricing, improve efficiency, or reallocate resources before it's too late to turn a profit.

4. Best Practices for Managing Jobs or Events

Here's how pros use Projects to stay ahead:

- Create Estimates at the Start: Give your customer a budget upfront and track how close you stay to it.
- Record ALL Costs to the Right Project: That includes small ones— parking, delivery fees, floral tape—every dollar counts.
- Avoid Double Entries: Don't log an expense both at the vendor level AND in the project manually. Tag it once, tag it right.
- Use Time Tracking Tools: If you bill for hours or assign team members to jobs, turn on time tracking and integrate with QuickBooks Time for even better accuracy.

- Review Often: Projects are dynamic—review your dashboards weekly to spot scope creep or unexpected costs.

With Projects in QuickBooks Online, you're not just tracking income and expenses—you're building clarity and control into every job. Whether you're a solo freelancer or managing a team of planners and vendors, this feature helps you make smarter decisions with less effort.

II. Workflow Automation Tools

Automation in QuickBooks Online isn't just a time-saver—it's a business upgrade. With workflow automation, you can stop chasing down reminders, approvals, or updates and let QuickBooks do the follow-up for you. Whether you're managing a growing team, juggling approvals, or simply want fewer things slipping through the cracks, workflows can bring consistency and peace of mind to your daily tasks.

1. What Workflow Automation Can Do for You

Think of workflows as your silent sidekick—handling reminders, sending nudges, and routing approvals, all in the background.

Here's what automation can help you with:

- Automatic Reminders – Remind your team (or yourself) to send estimates, deposit checks, or follow up on overdue invoices.
- Real-Time Notifications – Alert peers or managers when a vendor credit is created, a bill is updated, or a PO is approved.
- Streamlined Approvals – Create approval chains for bills, purchase orders, and invoices so nothing gets stuck waiting on someone's desk.

Real-world examples:

- Set an invoice approval workflow that routes invoices over $1,000 to a manager.
- Create a sales tax due reminder for the 15th of each month.
- Get notified when a vendor credit or expense is updated—perfect for audit trails.

2. Exploring the Workflow Template Library

To access the workflow template libary: click on Gear icon > Manage workflows under the Tool section.

Here are a few built-in workflows you'll find:

- Sales Tax Reminders – Never miss a deadline again.

- Notifications for PO, Bill, or Vendor Credit Updates – Keep your finance team looped in when changes are made.
- Invoice Follow-ups and Payment Reminders – Gently nudge customers for payment or prompt your team to follow up.
- Recurring Reports – Schedule key financial reports (like P&L or overdue invoices) to be sent automatically to the right people.
- Custom Alerts for Employees or Vendors – Birthdays, anniversaries, missing details—QuickBooks can handle the reminders.

Workflow templates

Notify about PO update	Schedule and send a report	Notify about Vendor Credit updated
Notify your peers / managers to review the PO you updated.	We will send reports at a frequency you choose.	Notify yourself / peers / managers about vendor credit updated.
Purchase Order Notification	Report	Vendor Credit Notification

Get sales tax due reminder	Send employee document reminder [NEW]	Notify about PO creation
Get reminder to pay sales tax on time.	Reminder for sending pending documents	Notify your peers / managers to review the PO you created.
Sales Tax Reminder	Employee Reminder	Purchase Order Notification

These templates are ready to go with just a few tweaks—and they're perfect for small teams that want to look big on process.

3. Customizing and Managing Workflows

Need something more specific? You can create or edit your own workflow to suit your business.

What would you like to automate in QuickBooks?

Select record for workflow

Invoice ∨

- ✓ Invoice
- Bill
- Bill payment
- Estimate
- Purchase order
- Statement
- Report

QuickBooks to do

Approval	Notification	Send	Update

Next

159

Here's how to make workflows work for you:

- Go to Gear icon > Manage workflows > Templates.
- Click + Custom Workflow or edit an existing one.
- Set your trigger event (e.g., invoice created, PO updated).

What would you like to automate in QuickBooks?

Select record for workflow

Invoice ⌄

Define action that you'd like QuickBooks to do

Reminder	Approval	Notification	Send	Update

- Click on the action window to edit and define the action that will be taken once trigger event occurs. Choose who should get notified and how.
- Adjust the conditions—like triggering only if a bill exceeds $500.

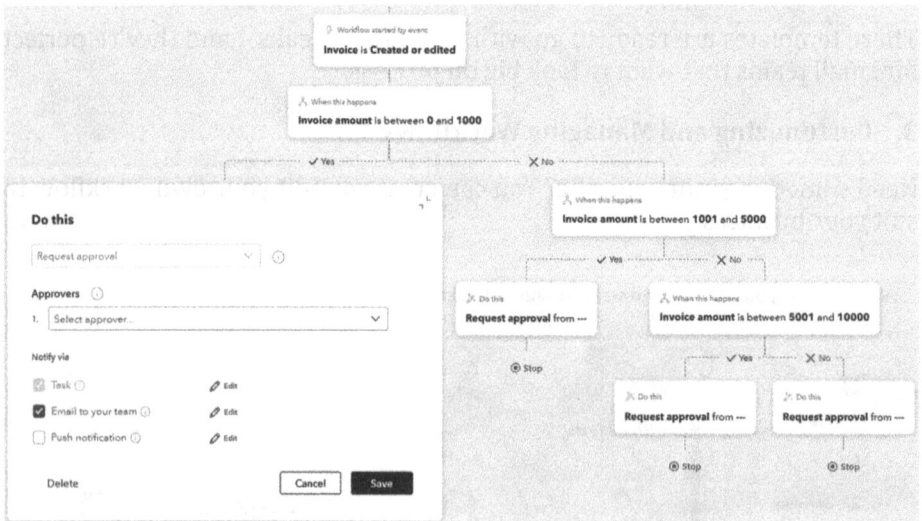

Once created, manage everything under My Workflows:

- Edit timing, recipients, or logic anytime.
- Use the History tab to review what actions your workflows performed (great for tracking and troubleshooting).

4. Approvals and Multi-Step Automation

Larger teams or more regulated industries often require approval chains—and QuickBooks supports that too.

Here's what you can automate:

- Invoice Approvals – Only send customer invoices after internal sign-off.
- Bill and Purchase Order Approvals – Route to specific approvers based on amount, vendor, or department.
- Multi-Step Routing – Add multiple approval conditions, like "If over $5,000, send to CFO," or "If assigned to Marketing, notify Marketing Lead."

With these tools, approvals are no longer bottlenecks—they're just smart workflows.

5. Tips to Avoid Workflow Overload

More automation is not always better. Too many alerts can quickly become noise. Here's how to keep it smart:

- Start small – Pick one area to automate, like invoice reminders or bill approvals.
- Audit your workflows quarterly – Turn off anything outdated or no longer useful.
- Test before scaling – Always run a few live tests before rolling automation across your team.

Tip: Use automation for consistency, not complexity. If a task is repeatable, predictable, and time-consuming, it's a great candidate for a workflow.

III. Advanced Accounting Tools (QuickBooks Online Advanced)

For businesses looking to scale operations with precision, QuickBooks Online Advanced delivers powerful tools that go beyond day-to-day bookkeeping. These features bring automation, compliance, and control together in one place—freeing you from spreadsheet chaos and giving you strategic oversight when it matters most.

1. Automating Revenue Recognition

If you handle long-term projects, subscription billing, or service contracts, chances are you can't recognize all your revenue right when the invoice goes out. That's where revenue recognition comes in.

What it is:

Revenue recognition ensures income is recorded in the period it's earned—not necessarily when it's received. This is essential for compliance with accounting standards like ASC 606, and it helps your financial reports accurately reflect business performance.

How QuickBooks helps:

With QBO Advanced, you can automate the entire process:

- Set custom recognition schedules—whether you recognize revenue monthly, quarterly, or in a custom pattern.
- Easily manage deferred vs. recognized revenue so you're not relying on external spreadsheets to track.
- Generate reports that align with GAAP standards and provide clean, audit-friendly documentation.

Automated recognition improves forecasting, giving you clarity on upcoming revenue and helping with decisions like staffing or investment.

2. Managing Fixed Assets in QBO

Got business vehicles, equipment, or machinery? Then you have fixed assets—and QuickBooks can help you manage them from purchase to retirement.

What's considered a fixed asset?

Think company-owned trucks, laptops, office furniture, or even heavy machinery. These are long-term assets that lose value over time, and tracking that depreciation is key for tax prep and accurate financials.

What you can do in QBO Advanced:

- Add individual fixed asset entries with purchase price, acquisition date, and expected lifespan.
- Automate depreciation schedules based on straight-line or custom rules.
- Easily generate Fixed Asset Summary Reports to see value, depreciation to date, and net book value—all in one place.

Why it matters: Automating depreciation helps ensure you're claiming the right deductions without over- or under-reporting asset value.

3. Advanced Permissions and Roles

When your business grows, more people start using QuickBooks—and not everyone needs to see everything. That's where custom user roles and permissions in QBO Advanced come in.

Here's how you can stay in control:

- Create roles like "Sales Manager," "Bookkeeper," or "Operations Assistant," and give access only to what they need.
- Limit visibility by department, location, or task type—protecting sensitive data like payroll or banking.
- Use audit logs to track who made what change and when—critical for accountability and fraud prevention.

Tip: Clear access control helps you delegate confidently while protecting your financial integrity.

IV. Bringing It All Together: Tips for Advanced Users

Whether you're already using QBO Advanced or thinking about leveling up, here's how to make the most of these premium tools.

1. When to Consider Upgrading

You might be ready for QBO Advanced if:

- You're managing multiple projects, departments, or team members.
- You need more automation and want to streamline approvals, reports, or revenue recognition.
- You want deeper insights with custom reporting, budgeting, and forecasting.

If your business is growing and your processes are getting more complex, QBO Advanced can bring the structure and automation to match.

2. Integrating Third-Party Tools

QBO Advanced plays nicely with others. With its open ecosystem, you can:

- Sync with CRMs like HubSpot or Salesforce for seamless lead-to-invoice workflows.
- Connect to project management tools like Trello or Asana for better task tracking.
- Automate via tools like Zapier, or sync apps from the App Store for specialized needs like inventory, payroll, or time tracking.

The result? A streamlined workflow from customer interaction to financial reporting.

3. Scaling With Confidence

As your business expands, so does the need for tighter systems. Here's how advanced features keep you agile:

- Use dashboards and KPIs to spot trends early.
- Leverage forecasting tools to guide investments and hiring.
- Delegate smarter with custom roles, confident that visibility is controlled.

These tools aren't just about efficiency—they're about making decisions with better data, protecting your business, and positioning for growth.

CHAPTER 9: CLOSING THE BOOKS AND SPECIAL TRANSACTIONS

I. Performing Monthly and Year-End Closing

Closing the books isn't just an accountant's ritual—it's your opportunity to review, reset, and move forward with clarity. Whether you're wrapping up the month or the entire year, QuickBooks Online gives you the tools to do it with confidence. In this section, we'll guide you through creating a repeatable process that ensures accuracy, avoids surprises, and gives you peace of mind.

1. Monthly Closing Checklist

At the end of each month, follow this simple checklist to keep your books tidy:

a. Review Undeposited Funds and Open Invoices

Start by checking the Undeposited Funds account. This account acts as a temporary holding area for payments you've received but haven't yet deposited to a bank account in QuickBooks.

- Go to Reports > Standard Reports > Balance Sheet, click the Undeposited funds balance, and confirm that each payment listed has either been deposited or properly applied.

- If the balance is growing or old transactions linger, it could indicate an incomplete workflow (e.g., invoice payments recorded but not deposited).

Compact | 100% ⌄   ○ ⊟ ⊜ ⊡ ⋮   ◇ 1 Insight

Balance Sheet
EverBloom Services
As of December 29, 2025

Account	Total
⌄ Assets	
⌄ Current Assets	
> Bank Accounts	$73,860.36
⌄ Accounts Receivable	
Accounts receivable	4,111.00
Total for Accounts Receivable	$4,111.00
⌄ Other Current Assets	
Inventory Asset	1,345.00
Undeposited funds	200.00

Next, head to Sales > Invoices and filter by Open Invoices.

- Follow up on overdue balances.
- Apply any payments received but not yet matched.
- Consider issuing statements to customers with outstanding balances.

An aging A/R report is your best friend here. It helps prioritize which customers to follow up with based on how long the invoice has been outstanding.

b. Review Unpaid Bills and Vendor Credits

Now it's time to take care of the vendor side of the house.

- Go to Expenses > Vendors or run the Accounts Payable Aging Summary report.
- Identify any bills that are due or overdue. This helps with cash flow planning and avoids late fees.
- Review outstanding vendor credits. If you've received refunds or discounts, be sure they're properly applied to related bills. Don't let credits sit unused—they're real money!

Best practice: Create a recurring reminder to follow up on credits quarterly, especially with vendors you use less frequently.

c. Match Bank Feeds and Categorize Transactions

Matching transactions from your bank feed is one of the most important steps in keeping your books clean.

- Go to Accounting > Bank transactions and make sure everything in the Pending tab is either matched, added, or categorized properly.
- Don't leave transactions hanging—it can lead to doubled income/ expenses or missed deductions.

When categorizing:

- Use rules for recurring charges (e.g., subscriptions, utilities).
- Split transactions when needed (e.g., a vendor invoice that covers multiple expense categories).

d. Reconcile Accounts Before Closing

Reconciliation is non-negotiable. Even if you're using bank feeds, transactions can be duplicated or missed.

- Go to Accounting > Reconcile, and work through each bank and credit card account.

- If the difference isn't zero, drill down to find what's missing or incorrect.

Tip: Reconciling cleared checks and automatic payments is a great way to catch fraudulent or erroneous activity early.

e. Run Key Monthly Reports

Finally, run a set of core financial reports to review your overall performance and spot issues:

- Profit and Loss: Check revenue trends, large expenses, or unusual spikes, gaps, or duplicated entries.
- Balance Sheet: Look for negative balances, unusual growth in liabilities, or changes in retained earnings.
- Accounts Receivable Aging Summary: Focus on slow-paying customers.
- Accounts Payable Aging Summary: Know what you owe—and when.

Recommendation: Save a PDF or export these reports monthly and store them securely. This creates a paper trail and supports long-term planning.

Monthly closings help you stay on top of your numbers and prevent issues from snowballing into bigger problems down the road.

2. Year-End Closing Procedures

The end of your fiscal year is more than just another month-end close—it's your opportunity to tie everything together, reflect on your performance, and start the new year with clarity. QuickBooks Online doesn't require traditional closing entries to roll your books into the new year, but as an experienced accountant would tell you, there are still key steps you should take to close out the year properly and ensure your financials are clean, complete, and tax-ready.

Let's walk through a responsible year-end closing process in QBO.

a. Review Retained Earnings and Closing Entries

QuickBooks Online automatically rolls your net income into Retained Earnings on your Balance Sheet once the new fiscal year begins. You won't see a journal entry for this—but you can (and should) understand what changed.

- Run your Profit and Loss report for the full fiscal year.
- Confirm that net income matches the change in retained earnings.
- If you or your accountant need to allocate year-end profit (e.g., dividends, owner's draw, or retained capital), you can record a manual journal entry.

Tip: If your books are on accrual basis, review revenue and expense cutoffs to ensure income and costs are booked in the correct period.

b. Archive and Back Up Key Reports

QuickBooks is cloud-based and autosaves everything, but for year-end, it's smart to archive a snapshot of your financials—especially for historical comparison and audits. Create and download/export these reports:

- Profit and Loss (Yearly and by Month)
- Balance Sheet
- Statement of Cash Flows
- Accounts Receivable and Payable Aging
- Inventory Valuation Summary (if applicable)
- General Ledger (for the full year)

You can also invite your accountant as a QBO user or share an Accountant's Copy, allowing them to access what they need without data duplication.

c. Lock the Books to Prevent Accidental Changes

Once you've finalized the year, protect your records by locking your books. This ensures no one can unintentionally change a prior-period transaction that would throw off your reports. To lock your books:

- Go to Gear icon > Account and Settings > Advanced.
- Under Accounting, toggle on the Closing the books setting and set a closing date.
- Choose whether to allow changes with a password (recommended for shared files).

Accounting		
First month of fiscal year ⑦		January ▾
First month of income tax year		Same as fiscal year ▾
Accounting method ⑦		Accrual ▾
Close the books ⑦		⬤
Closing date		
12/31/2025		
Allow changes after viewing a warning ▾ ⑦		
Cancel Save		

This is an essential control that protects your data integrity—especially if you have multiple users.

d. Post Year-End Adjustments (Accruals, Depreciation, etc.)

While QBO automates many tasks, year-end adjustments often require a human touch. Work with your accountant to:

- Record accrued expenses (like unpaid utilities or wages).
- Adjust prepaid expenses and unearned revenue.
- Post depreciation entries using your accountant's calculations or fixed asset schedules.
- Clean up clearing accounts or reconcile accounts that should zero out.

Use the +New > Journal Entry tool for these adjustments, and always leave clear memos and references for audit clarity.

Note: These entries are often the final touch before handing off your books to a tax preparer.

e. Why Year-End Closing Matters

Your year-end close is about more than taxes—it's about clarity, compliance, and confidence going into the next year. With clean records and reliable reports:

- Your tax filings will be smoother.
- Your budget for the new year will be better grounded.
- Your financial decisions will be smarter and faster.

The year-end close gives you a fresh slate. When done right, it sets you up for stronger strategy, tighter controls, and more peace of mind—no matter what the new year brings.

3. Reviewing and Adjusting Financial Records

Before you can close the books with confidence, it's essential to give your records one last detailed review. This step is where seasoned accountants catch what automated systems might miss—small errors, misclassifications, or overlooked transactions that can snowball into big reporting discrepancies. Adjusting your books now saves headaches later, especially during tax filing or audits.

a. Spot and Correct Common Posting Errors

Let's face it—mistakes happen. But the key is catching them before the year is closed. Here are a few common culprits to investigate:

- Duplicate transactions (especially if syncing with bank feeds and manually entering some records).
- Transactions posted to the wrong account, such as meals coded to office supplies or credit card payments accidentally posted as expenses.
- Negative balances in asset or liability accounts, which often signal setup or entry issues.
- Invoices or bills with no associated payment or expense, indicating incomplete records.

To check:

- Run a General Ledger report filtered for the year.
- Use the Transaction Detail by Account report to drill into specific accounts.

Make corrections by editing the original transaction, not by making adjusting journal entries unless absolutely necessary.

b. Review Suspense Accounts and Uncategorized Transactions

If you've used Uncategorized Expense, or Uncategorized Asset, now is the time to deal with them.

To do this:

- Navigate to Reports > Profit & Loss or Balance Sheet.
- Look for any generic or temporary accounts with balances.
- Click the dollar amount to open the list of transactions.
- Reassign each one to the correct chart of accounts category, vendor, or customer.

c. Adjust Owner Draws, Distributions, and Equity Balances

In small businesses—especially sole proprietorships, LLCs, and S Corps—owner contributions and withdrawals don't always follow a formal payroll process. That's where owner's equity accounts come in.

Here's what to check:

- Review all transactions posted to personal expense or draw accounts.
- Confirm that personal expenses weren't accidentally coded to business expense accounts (and vice versa).
- If your accountant needs to reclassify year-end profits into retained earnings or owner's equity accounts, use a journal entry with a memo.
- For partnerships or multi-member LLCs, ensure each owner's capital

account reflects the correct balance based on distributions and earnings.

By thoroughly reviewing and adjusting your financial records, you're doing more than just tidying up—you're safeguarding the financial integrity of your business. And that's what sets a proactive business owner apart.

II. Reconciling Bank and Credit Card Accounts

1. Understanding Account Reconciliation

Reconciling your bank and credit card accounts isn't just another item on your to-do list—it's one of the most critical practices for maintaining trustworthy books. Reconciliation is your financial reality check: it ensures the transactions in QuickBooks Online match what actually happened in your bank or credit card accounts. When done consistently and correctly, reconciliation protects your business from costly errors, fraud, and tax-time surprises.

a. Why Reconciliation Is Vital to Financial Integrity

Bank feeds are powerful, but they're not foolproof.

- Some transactions might not import automatically—like older entries or adjustments.
- Duplicates can sneak in if you manually record a payment or deposit before the bank feed syncs it.
- Bank errors or unauthorized charges may go unnoticed unless you're reviewing every line.

Reconciliation gives you the chance to verify each transaction line by line. You're not just reviewing what's been recorded—you're confirming that what's in your books aligns perfectly with what your financial institution reports. That's peace of mind, and it's essential for tax prep, reporting accuracy, and fraud prevention.

b. What Accounts Should You Reconcile?

While bank accounts are the most commonly reconciled, don't stop there. You should reconcile:

- Checking and savings accounts
- Credit card accounts
- PayPal or other payment platforms
- Petty cash (if tracked as an account in QuickBooks)
- Loan and line-of-credit accounts (optional but recommended for tracking payments and interest)

c. Common Reasons for Reconciliation Discrepancies

Issue	What It Means	How to Fix
Missing transactions	A deposit, withdrawal, or payment wasn't entered into QuickBooks.	Review your bank statement and add the missing entry manually.
Duplicate entries	The same transaction is recorded twice—often once manually and once via bank feed.	Delete or exclude the duplicate transaction.
Incorrect dates	A transaction has the wrong date, so it doesn't match the bank statement.	Edit the transaction to match the correct statement date.
Wrong amounts	A typo or incorrect entry was made.	Adjust the amount to reflect the correct value from your statement.
Uncleared items from prior months	Transactions marked as uncleared months ago haven't been reconciled.	Investigate these. They may be voided checks or errors needing correction.

Reconciliation may sound like a formality, but it's the heartbeat of accurate bookkeeping. When your accounts are properly reconciled, you can trust your numbers—and make smarter, faster business decisions with confidence.

2. Step-by-Step Bank Reconciliation in QuickBooks

Here's how to get it done:

1. Gather Your Bank Statement:
   » Grab your latest bank or credit card statement. You'll need the statement ending date and the ending balance.

2. Start Reconciliation:
   » Go to Accounting > Reconcile.
   » Choose the account you want to reconcile.
   » Enter the statement ending date and ending balance, then click Start Reconciling.

3. Match Transactions:
   » QuickBooks shows you a list of transactions.
   » Check off each one that appears on your statement.
   » Use filters or the search bar to find specific transactions.

Reconcile   Checking

Statement ending date: April 20, 2025

Edit info	Finish now ⌄

$4,486.85
STATEMENT ENDING BALANCE

–

$4,486.85
CLEARED BALANCE

✅ **$0.00**
DIFFERENCE

$5,000.00
BEGINNING BALANCE

–

$1,537.15
8 PAYMENTS

+

$1,024.00
3 DEPOSITS

⌃ Show me around

▽ ✕ Statement ending date   Clear filter / View all | Payments | Deposits | **All** | 🖨 ⚙

DATE ▲	CLEARED DATE	TYPE	REF NO.	ACCOUNT	PAYEE	MEMO	📎	PAYMENT (USD)	DEPOSIT (USD) ▲
03/03/2025		Sales Receipt	1008	Design income	Kate Whelan				225.00
03/05/2025		Receive Payment		Accounts Receivable (A/R)	Amy's Bird Sanct...	Amy claims the p...			105.00
03/07/2025		Bill Payment	7	Accounts Payable (A/P)	Hicks Hardware			250.00	
03/10/2025		Expense	8	Landscaping Services:Job M...	Hicks Hardware			24.36	
03/19/2025		Cash Expense		Automobile	Squeaky Kleen C...			19.99	
03/19/2025		Cash Expense		Meals and Entertainment	Bob's Burger Joint			5.66	
03/19/2025		Check		Legal & Professional Fees:La...	Tony Rondonuwu			100.00	
03/20/2025		Check	70	Maintenance and Repair	Chin's Gas and Oil			185.00	
03/20/2025		Cash Expense		Automobile:Fuel	Chin's Gas and Oil			52.14	
03/21/2025		Bill Payment	11	Accounts Payable (A/P)	Hall Properties			900.00	
03/21/2025		Receive Payment	1886	Accounts Receivable (A/R)	Cool Cars				694.00

4. Watch the Difference:

» The goal is to get the difference at the top of the screen to $0.00.

» If the difference isn't zero, there's likely a missing or incorrect transaction.

5. Finish and Save:

» When the difference is $0.00, click Finish Now.

» You'll see a Reconciliation Report—save or print it for your records.

3. Reconciling Credit Card Statements Accurately

Reconciling credit cards works just like bank accounts, but with some tips:

- Make sure interest charges are recorded:

» Use + Create > Expense to enter any interest or fees that don't show in your feed.

- Split payments if needed:

» If you made a partial payment, be sure to match it accurately when reconciling.

- Paying off balances:

» When you pay off a credit card, ensure the payment is recorded properly in both accounts so you don't end up with a mismatch.

Accuracy with credit cards helps keep liabilities straight and avoids throwing off your expense reports.

III. Recording Journal Entries and Adjustments

While most of your day-to-day entries in QuickBooks Online happen automatically through invoices, expenses, and bank feeds, there are times when you need to make manual adjustments. That's where journal entries come in. These powerful tools allow you (or your accountant) to fine-tune your books for accuracy. Don't worry—it's not as intimidating as it sounds. We'll walk you through the what, why, and how.

1. Basics of Journal Entries

A journal entry is a manual transaction that adjusts balances between accounts. You might use one to record depreciation, correct an error, or handle complex accruals. Each journal entry must always be in balance—meaning total debits equal total credits.

Common uses include:

- Recording payroll corrections
- Adjusting for prepaid expenses or deferred revenue
- Entering depreciation on fixed assets
- Reclassifying income or expenses

Even if you're not an accountant, understanding the basics of journal entries can help you catch up or clean up your books like a pro.

2. Creating and Editing Journal Entries in QuickBooks

Create a Journal Entry

1. Navigate to the Journal Entry Screen:
   - » Click + Create > Journal Entry.

2. Enter the Journal Date:
   - » Use the date the adjustment should affect.
   - » For year-end entries, use the last day of your fiscal year.

3. Add the First Line (Debit):
   - » Choose the account you want to debit (e.g., Insurance Expense).
   - » Enter the amount and optional memo.

4. Add the Second Line (Credit):
   - » Choose the account to credit (e.g., Prepaid Insurance).
   - » Enter the same amount to balance the entry.

5. Assign Classes or Locations (if applicable):

» Helpful for tracking departmental or regional performance.

6. Save the Entry:

» Click Save and Close or Save and New to create another.

Journal date			Journal no.				
04/24/2025 📅			1				

#	ACCOUNT	DEBITS	CREDITS	DESCRIPTION	NAME	STORE	
⠿ 1	Insurance	$50.00		Property Insurance Expense			🗑
⠿ 2	Prepaid expenses		$50.00	Property Insurance Expense			🗑

Create a Recurring Journal Entries

If you're posting the same entry each month (like depreciation or accruals), you can make the journal entry recurring:

- After creating the journal entry, click Make Recurring at the bottom of the screen.
- Choose the frequency, start date, and end date (if applicable).
- Give it a name and save the template.

🕐 **Journal Entry #1**   ⚙ ⑦ ✕

Recurring Journal Entry

Template name	Type				
Insurance Allocation	Scheduled ∨	Create	1	days in advance	

Interval						Start date	End	
Monthly ∨	on	day ∨	1st ∨	of every	1 month(s)	MM/DD/YYYY 📅	None ∨	

💬 Feedback

#	ACCOUNT	DEBITS	CREDITS	DESCRIPTION	NAME	STORE	
⠿ 1	Insurance	$50.00		Property Insurance Expense			🗑
⠿ 2	Prepaid expenses		$50.00	Property Insurance Expense			🗑

Editing a Journal Entry:

- Go to Reports > Standard Reports > Journal, find the entry, and click to open and edit.

Be careful—editing journal entries after reconciliation may throw off your books. If unsure, check with your accountant first.

3. Making Adjusting Entries for Accruals and Prepaid Expenses

Whether you run your books on a cash or accrual basis, there are moments when timing differences arise—this is where adjusting journal entries shine. Some of the most important journal entries are those that align income and expenses with the correct period.

a. Accruing Unpaid Expenses

Accruals: Used to record expenses that have been incurred but not yet paid

Let's say your vendor sent an invoice for December services, but you haven't received the bill yet—and your books need to reflect the cost before year-end. You'd create a journal entry like this:

- Debit: Expense account (e.g., Professional Fees) | Credit: Accounts Payable
- Later, when the bill arrives, you can match it against this liability.

b. Deferring Revenue or Expenses

If a customer prepaid you for a service to be performed in a future period, you shouldn't recognize that as income just yet.

- Debit: Bank (for the deposit) | Credit: Unearned Revenue (a liability account)
- Then, once you've delivered the service, reverse the entry.
- Debit: Unearned Revenue | Credit: Revenue

Similarly, prepaid expenses like insurance or rent should be recorded as assets first, then expensed out monthly.

c. Reclassifying Prepaid Assets

If you paid $1,200 for a 12-month insurance policy in January, you'd record it initially as:

- Debit: Prepaid Insurance | Credit: Bank Account (initial payment)
- Then, monthly: Debit: Insurance Expense | Credit: Prepaid Insurance

d. Depreciation of assets

Depreciation Entries: To reflect asset wear and tear over time.

- Debit: Depreciation Expense | Credit: Accumulated Depreciation

These adjustments ensure your financial reports reflect the real financial health of your business—matching income and expenses to the correct period.

Journal entries might seem technical at first, but once you understand when and how to use them, they become an essential part of closing the books accurately. Whether you're fixing an error, making a year-end adjustment, or preparing for tax season, this skill gives you a whole new level of control.

IV. Managing Loans, Lines of Credit, and Bad Debt

Sometimes business requires outside financing or tough decisions about unpaid invoices. Whether you're taking out a loan, using a credit line, or writing off a bad debt, QuickBooks Online has your back. In this section, we'll break down how to handle each of these scenarios so your books stay accurate and your financial picture stays clear.

1. Setting Up Loan Accounts and Credit Lines in QuickBooks

Recording a loan in QuickBooks is essential for tracking what you owe and how you're repaying it.

1. Create a Loan Liability Account:
   » Go to Accounting > Chart of Accounts > New.
   » Choose Long Term Liabilities > Other Long Term Liabilities (or Other Current Liabilities if short-term).
   » Name it (e.g., "Business Loan - Bank of XYZ").

2. Record the Loan Deposit:
   » Go to + Create > Journal Entry.
   » Debit: Bank Account (where the funds were deposited).
   » Credit: Loan Liability Account (for the total loan amount).

3. Set Up a Recurring Loan Payment (Optional):
   » Use + Create > Expense or + Create > Check to record payments.
   » Split the payment:
      » Debit: Loan Liability (principal portion)
      » Debit: Interest Expense (interest portion)
      » Credit: Bank Account (total payment)

Having a clear loan account ensures you can track your outstanding balance and interest costs over time.

2. Recording Loan Disbursements and Interest Payments

Whenever you make a payment on your loan or draw from a line of credit:

- Use the original liability account to reduce the balance owed.

- Separate the interest from the principal to maintain accurate expense reporting.
- Add memos or attachments (like loan statements) for easy reference.

You can also use Recurring Transactions to simplify fixed monthly loan payments.

3. Tracking Outstanding Balances

QuickBooks doesn't automatically generate loan amortization schedules, but you can track balances manually or with an Excel sheet.

1. Use Reports to Monitor Activity:

   » Go to Reports > Standard Reports > Transaction Detail by Account and filter by your loan account.

   » This shows all payments and balances over time.

2. Optional: Use a third-party amortization calculator to break down payments by month and create a schedule.

   » Manually match QuickBooks entries to the schedule to ensure accuracy.

Tracking your loan balance helps ensure that every dollar is accounted for—and keeps lenders happy, too.

4. Managing and Writing Off Uncollectible Invoices

Sometimes a customer just doesn't pay. When that happens, you'll need to write off the invoice properly to keep your accounts receivable clean.

1. Create a Bad Debt Expense Account (If Needed):

   » Go to Settings > Chart of Accounts > New.

   » Select Expenses > Bad Debt.

2. Create a Credit Memo:

   » Go to + Create > Credit Memo.

   » Select the customer and the original product/service.

   » Use Bad Debt as the income or expense account.

3. Apply the Credit to the Invoice:

   » Go to + Create > Receive Payment.

   » Choose the customer and apply the credit memo to the open invoice.

This removes the unpaid invoice from your books and records it as a loss—keeping your financials accurate and honest.

Dealing with loans and unpaid invoices is part of running a business—but with QuickBooks Online and the right approach, it doesn't have to be stressful. These tools give you full visibility into what you owe, what you've paid, and what's no longer collectible. Best of all, they help you stay focused on the big picture.

V. Preparing for Tax Season Efficiently

Tax time doesn't need to be stressful—especially when you've got QuickBooks Online and a well-prepared plan. The more organized you are, the easier it is for your accountant (or yourself!) to file accurate returns, uncover tax-saving opportunities, and avoid costly errors. This section walks you through the key steps to get your books tax-ready—from compiling the right documents to working hand-in-hand with your accountant like a pro.

a. Gathering Necessary Financial Documents

Here's what you (and your accountant) will need to begin preparing your return:

- Profit & Loss Statement (P&L): Your go-to report for taxable income. Run it for both the full fiscal year and key comparative periods (like Q4).
- Balance Sheet: A snapshot of assets, liabilities, and equity—crucial for depreciation, loans, and retained earnings review.
- Trial Balance: This report gives your accountant a quick reference of all accounts and balances—perfect for finding errors and verifying the books.
- Payroll Reports: Include wage summaries, tax withholdings, and year-end forms like W-2s or 940/941 filings.
- 1099 Contractor Payments: Run a 1099 Transaction Detail report to ensure you're capturing all applicable non-employee compensation.
- Receipts & Documentation: Any deductible expenses should have a receipt or record to back it up. Make sure your QuickBooks receipt capture or document storage is up-to-date.

Tip: Create a "Tax Season" folder on your desktop or in Google Drive with all reports and backups. Share access with your accountant to streamline collaboration.

b. Reviewing and Finalizing Financial Reports

Before sending anything to your accountant, take a few moments to validate the accuracy of your reports:

- Compare YTD Actuals to Prior Years: Unexpected jumps or drops in revenue or expenses should be reviewed—are they accurate or a result of misclassification?

- Compare Against Budget (if available): If you've created a budget, compare actual performance and investigate major variances.

- Review Account Balances: Pay close attention to:

  » Large or unusual balances in Uncategorized Income/Expenses.

  » Negative balances in asset or liability accounts (often a red flag).

  » Equity balances that need to be clarified (especially if you took draws/distributions).

- Clean Up Open Items: Clear out unapplied credits, unapplied payments, or duplicate transactions that could throw off your financials.

c. Exporting and Backing Up Data for Tax Preparation

Backups and data access should never be an afterthought. Even if you're working entirely in QuickBooks Online, it's a good habit to export your key data for archival purposes—and it's helpful to your tax preparer too.

- Export the General Ledger and Journal Reports: These reports provide full transaction details and are essential for your accountant's deeper review or audits.

- Download Year-End Reports:

  » Profit and Loss

  » Balance Sheet

  » Trial Balance

  » A/R and A/P Aging

  » Payroll summaries (if using QBO Payroll)

- Accountant Access: If your tax professional uses QuickBooks Accountant, invite them under Settings > Manage Users > Accounting Firms. This gives them real-time access and specialized tools to make adjustments without disturbing your work.

- Export an Accountant Copy: If they prefer offline work, export your reports as Excel files or PDFs and share them securely via a shared drive or encrypted email.

d. Coordinating with Your Accountant

A smooth tax season hinges on proactive communication with your accountant. Set expectations early and keep the lines of communication open.

- Create a Year-End Checklist: Include all key documents, login credentials (if applicable), and important notes about your books.

- Clarify Any Adjustments Made After Year-End: If you made edits in January for the previous year, be sure to notify your accountant so nothing is missed.
- Provide Context for Journal Entries or Unusual Items: A short explanation goes a long way. For example:
  » "We wrote off a $2,000 invoice for a client that filed bankruptcy."
  » "Purchased a new delivery van in December using financing—see journal entry."
- Ask for Recommendations: Don't be afraid to ask your accountant about improving your processes, maximizing deductions, or fixing recurring issues.

e. Year-End Tax Planning Tips

Proactive tax planning beats last-minute scrambling—every time. Here are a few smart strategies you or your accountant may consider implementing before finalizing the return:

- Evaluate Owner Draws vs. Salaries:
  » If you're an S-Corp, ensure your salary meets IRS reasonable compensation requirements.
  » Compare how distributions or guaranteed payments were handled.
- Accelerate or Defer Income/Expenses:
  » Consider whether to push income into the next year or prepay expenses (like software or subscriptions) to reduce this year's taxable income.
  » Be mindful of cash flow before doing so.
- Review Capital Purchases for Depreciation:
  » Did you buy new equipment, furniture, or vehicles?
  » Discuss Section 179 or bonus depreciation opportunities with your tax pro.
- Confirm W-2s and 1099s Are Filed Accurately and On Time:
  » Ensure all employee and contractor data is current.
  » File on or before the IRS deadline to avoid penalties.

Tip: Start your year-end planning conversation in Q4—before the books are closed and it's too late to take action.

Conclusion: Continuing Your QuickBooks Journey

First off—congratulations! You've made it through a comprehensive journey that covered everything from setting up your QuickBooks Online account to handling payroll, reports, integrations, and even year-end tax prep. Whether you're a small business owner, a new bookkeeper, or someone eager to gain financial clarity, you've now got a rock-solid foundation.

But this is just the beginning.

1. Staying Updated with QuickBooks Changes

QuickBooks Online is always evolving. Features improve, interfaces refresh, and new tools are added regularly. Here's how to stay ahead:

- Explore the What's New Section: QuickBooks often highlights updates directly on your dashboard.
- Subscribe to Intuit's Newsletters: They provide useful insights and announcements.
- Join the QuickBooks Community: Visit forums, join webinars, and follow QBO influencers for real-world tips.
- Check In Monthly: Make it a habit to explore new features and updates every few weeks.

Learning QuickBooks is like learning any powerful tool—it gets easier (and more exciting!) the more you use it.

2. When and How to Get Professional Help

There's no shame in calling in the pros—especially when you're doing complex tax planning or filing, you need help cleaning up old data, or you just want a second set of eyes to review your books.

How to Find the Right Help:

- Use the "Find a ProAdvisor" tool on Intuit's website to locate certified QuickBooks experts near you.
- Ask your network for accountant recommendations.
- Choose someone who not only knows accounting, but also understands QBO inside and out.

The best professionals won't just fix issues—they'll teach you how to avoid them.

Remember: mastering your finances doesn't happen in one sitting. It happens through repetition, curiosity, and smart habits. This book was designed to give you confidence, clarity, and control—and now you've got all three.

Keep logging in. Keep learning. Keep growing. Your business deserves a strong financial foundation—and now, you've built it.

Here's to your continued success with QuickBooks Online—and beyond!

APPENDIX: GLOSSARY OF ESSENTIAL ACCOUNTING AND QUICKBOOKS TERMS

Understanding financial language is a huge step forward in mastering your bookkeeping and business management in QuickBooks Online. This glossary is designed for beginners and business owners who might be new to accounting. It includes the most essential terms you'll encounter, explained in clear, everyday language.

A

Accounts Payable (A/P) – Money your business owes to suppliers or vendors.

Accounts Receivable (A/R) – Money customers owe your business.

Accrual Basis Accounting – Records income and expenses when they're earned or incurred—not when money moves.

Asset – Anything valuable your business owns, like cash, inventory, or equipment.

B

Balance Sheet – A snapshot of your business's financial position at a moment in time: assets, liabilities, and equity.

Bank Reconciliation – Matching your bank statement with QuickBooks records.

Bill – A record of money owed to a vendor.

Budget – A financial plan to guide spending and income.

C

Cash Flow – Tracks money coming in vs. going out.

Chart of Accounts – A list of categories used to track financial transactions.

Cost of Goods Sold (COGS) – Direct costs of producing goods or services you sell.

Credit Memo – A reduction in what a customer owes, often for returns or discounts.

D

Deferred Revenue – Payment received before services or products are delivered.

Depreciation – Spreading the cost of a large asset (like a van) over time.

Double-Entry Accounting – Every transaction impacts at least two accounts to keep your books balanced.

E

Equity – Your business's value after subtracting liabilities from assets.

Estimate – A quote you send to a customer before invoicing.

Expense – Money spent to operate your business.

F

Fixed Asset – Long-term resources like vehicles or machinery.

FUTA – Federal tax employers pay to support unemployment benefits.

I

Income Statement (Profit & Loss) – Shows how much you earned and spent over a period.

Inventory – Items you plan to sell; QuickBooks can track quantity and cost.

Invoice – A request for payment after delivering a product or service.

J

Journal Entry – A manual entry used to adjust balances or record special transactions.

L

Liability – Money your business owes, like loans or credit card debt.

Loan Payable – A specific type of liability for borrowed money.

M

Matching Principle – An accounting rule to record expenses in the same period as related income.

Memo – A note attached to a transaction for clarity.

N

Net Income – What's left after expenses are subtracted from income.

O

Opening Balance – The starting amount in an account when you begin tracking it in QuickBooks.

Owner's Draw – Money taken out of the business by the owner.

P

Payroll – Paying employees, including wages, taxes, and benefits.

Prepaid Expense – Expenses paid ahead of time, such as insurance.

Purchase Order (PO) – A document sent to a vendor to request goods/services.

R

Reconciliation – Ensuring QuickBooks matches your bank records.

Retained Earnings – Past profits kept in the business instead of being paid out.

S

Sales Receipt – Documented proof of a sale when payment is made immediately.

Statement of Cash Flows – Shows how money enters and leaves your business.

Suspense Account – Temporary placeholder for uncategorized transactions.

T

Taxable Sales – Sales that require charging sales tax.

Trial Balance – A list showing the balance of all accounts to check if debits and credits match.

U

Undeposited Funds – A temporary account holding customer payments that haven't been deposited yet.

V

Vendor – A person or company your business pays for goods or services.

Vendor Credit – A credit from a vendor for returned goods or overpayments.

W

W-2 – A form showing an employee's earnings and taxes withheld.

W-9 – A form you collect from contractors so you can issue a 1099 at year-end.

Write-Off – Removing an amount from your books, typically when it can't be collected.

BONUS

Thank you for purchasing the book! As a special token of our appreciation, I'm excited to offer you some free exclusive bonus resources of this guide.

Simply scan the QR code below to access or click on the link (if you are reading the eBook version).

Link: Bonus

Thanks again for trusting me as your guide. I'm wishing you every success as you take control of your business finances—one step, one click, one smart decision at a time.

With gratitude,

Ethan Wells

www.ingramcontent.com/pod-product-compliance
Lightning Source LLC
Chambersburg PA
CBHW071607210326
41597CB00019B/3433